LAST WISH

BETTY ROLLIN

WINGS BOOKS

New York • Avenel, New Jersey

Copyright © 1985 by Betty Rollin
Introduction copyright © 1996 by Betty Rollin

This 1996 edition is published by Wings Books,
a division of Random House Value Publishing, Inc.,
40 Engelhard Avenue, Avenel, New Jersey 07001,
by arrangement with the author.

Wings Books and colophon are trademarks of Random House Value
Publishing, Inc.

Random House
New York • Toronto • London • Sydney • Auckland

Printed and bound in the United States of America

Library of Congress Cataloging-in-Publication Data

Rollin, Betty.
        Last wish / by Betty Rollin.
                p. cm.
        ISBN 0-517-14935-4
        1. Rollin, Ida, 1908-1983—Death and burial. 2. Assisted suicide.
3. Ovaries—Cancer—Patients—United States—Biography. I. Title.
R726.R54 1996
362.1'9699465—dc20
[B]   95-44983
                                                             CIP

8 7 6 5 4 3 2 1

Introduction

I never set out to write a book about an issue. I wanted to write what struck me as a powerful story about a woman who happened to be my mother. To this day, I can't get over what she did and how she did it. There is inherent drama in any death, but a chosen death—this kind of chosen death, not the result of depression or misery, but of reason and pluck—had a kind of majesty about it. My mother was, in many ways, an ordinary, feet-on-the-ground woman. But at her death she soared. Mostly, I wrote the book because I was proud of her.

And I suppose I had some sense of mission about it. I knew—as did my mother—that she could not be the only terminally-ill person who wanted out of life and who couldn't get there without help. "What do people do who don't have children?" she asked me, not idly, once she knew we would help her to die. As alone as we felt with our struggle, we knew we were not alone. But little did we know how many people, how many families were going through the same agony—enough to start a movement. Because the right-to-die movement grew—and has grown—not from intellectual theory but from the heart.

A decade ago, when this book was first published, the Hemlock Society had a thousand or so members. Today, it has about forty thousand. And there are many other groups* and individuals who, with mercy and common sense in mind, favor some form of euthanasia—from Dr. Kevorkian (who some see as a loose cannon, but who has probably brought more attention to this issue than anyone) to those who think it would be nice if physicians paid a little more attention to Living Wills. Two attempts at getting state laws changed to allow physician aid-in-dying failed (narrowly) in Washington and California. But in 1994, Oregon voters passed an initiative that allows physicians, not to assist actively in the death of terminally-ill patients, but to prescribe a lethal dosage of drugs, allowing patients—who can swallow—to take their own lives. At this writing, however, legal challenges have prevented the measure from taking effect. About ten other states are in various stages of drafting legislation.

And here's a nice irony: As a result of the controversy about legal aid-in-dying, pain has gotten a lot more attention. Under-medication for pain has been an ongoing fact in most hospitals, but suddenly physicians arguing against assisted death on the grounds that "we can keep people comfortable" were now obliged to do so—or at least to do better.

As any movement grows, so inevitably does the disagreement among its participants. But the people I've met who want the notion of "death with dignity" to be a legal right often share that one thing which has both radicalized and united them: experience. Many have witnessed a prolonged,

* eg.: The Death With Dignity Education Center, Americans for Death With Dignity, Compassion in Dying

horrible death—a mother, a father, a wife, husband or child. Some have witnessed—or participated in—a ghastly attempt at suicide that failed. Some have been tormented with guilt for having helped someone they love to die. Some have been tormented with guilt for refusing to help someone they love to die. They've been there. And when you've been there, you change. As I have changed.

Suffering is just a word until you feel it. Or see someone you love feeling it. I've often thought that people who are against legal aid-in-dying are less cruel than they are inexperienced. Many people, luckier than they know, have never had their bodies turn into torture chambers. Many people believe the myth that pain can (always) be stopped by drugs. Drugs are amazing, but they don't work equally well on everybody. And besides, my mother would say if she were still here, don't forget about nausea—as bad as pain and often untreatable. I have received many letters since writing *Last Wish*. They are from people who have Been Through It and implicit in their letters is a question: If someone is at the end of life and is suffering terribly and is alert and sane and begs to die, why can't our society figure out a way to help?

I do believe that most patients, given the opportunity to end their lives, wouldn't. The wish to live is powerful, even under the most terrible—and hopeless—circumstances. But knowing that the option exists is, in itself, merciful. Many people I hear from are not sick, but they are afraid, afraid of being "strung up" by the technology and left to live and suffer. They are afraid of being trapped in life with no way out. My mother got out. But she knew she was lucky. She wanted others to have the same opportunity. And in her memory, so do I.

Betty Rollin
March 1996

1

chapter

Two hours before my mother killed herself, I noticed she had put on makeup. This shocked me, but it shouldn't have. Whatever the occasion, my mother liked to look her best. That was her way. Just as it was her way to die as she did—not when death summoned her, but when she summoned death.

She would have preferred to do her summoning alone, without help. But she had reason to ask for help. And when she did, I gave it.

The illness that made her want out of life was ovarian cancer, one of the sneakiest malignancies a body can house. That's why ovarian cancer is so deadly. Unlike a breast tumor, an ovarian tumor can't be detected except by gynecological examination and by that time it's often too late. That is, a metastasis—a spread—has already occurred.

The disease first struck my mother in the spring of 1981, two and a half years before she died. At least that's when she became aware of it. There was no way to know when it really began.

My mother's diagnosis was especially long in coming because of her intractable sense of the world as an orderly place. She knew as well as anyone else about the cruel, topsy-turvy things that happened to people. She read newspapers and watched the news on television. But no house of hers had ever burned to the ground, no child of hers had ever been hit by a drunk driver, and the one time in my thirties when I did have a serious illness, she took my recovery for granted. My mother had never been leveled by life, and she believed with all her heart that if you did things right they came out right.

When it came to matters of sickness and health, doing things right meant eating right, and of course she knew exactly what eating right was. As far back as the 1930s she took courses in nutrition, and nothing short of a wedding or a four-car collision stood in the way of her tuning in to Carlton Fredericks, the Ronald Colman of nutritionists, on the radio each week. In later years she moved on to Nathan Pritikin, whose sermons between hard covers occupied a place of honor on her coffee table alongside the books of her daughter and son-in-law.

Throughout my childhood, my father and I—in my mother's presence we were more like siblings than parent and child—sat, backs straight, at the dining table in our small, tidy house in Yonkers, New York, and assumed our roles as the beneficiaries of my mother's commitment to nutritional excellence.

Unbuttered brussels sprouts went uncontested in my mother's house, as did sugarless desserts—something thin and brown that passed for a cookie was doled out only on occasion—and the sun rarely set without a baked potato whose garnish was a command, "Eat the skin! The skin's the best part!"

My father had immigrated to the United States from Russia in 1919 with the usual difficulties and thereafter wanted no more from life than an absence of trouble. So he pretended to like what he found on his dinner plate every evening, and until I went to camp and found out about french fries and chocolate pudding, I didn't know any better. But camp came too late. By that time I was my mother's girl. Aside from their wickedness, french fries did nothing to excite my puritanical palate. And in the years that followed the story was the same. Whenever I tried to be a normal kid and eat junk, I couldn't. I didn't like it and I still don't.

My mother may have been right. My father and I both developed digestive systems that could have won prizes. And as other men his age began to complain about this pain and that ache, my father complained of nothing. Perhaps that was just his nature. He was such a jolly soul—a resolute viewer of life's bright side. It probably helped, though, that he never got sick. Unless you count the explosion in his heart which killed him in an instant at the age of seventy-two when he rose from his chair early one evening to turn the dial on the television set from Channel 2 to Channel 4.

My mother was not impressed. "My Leon died healthy," she said through her grief. The way he ate, she figured, how could he not be healthy? She couldn't get over how one organ, his heart, could have been impervious to all those green vegetables, all that sole broiled dry, all those skins of all those baked potatoes.

By the same token, six years later, she couldn't fathom how she herself could have cancer when her own eating habits were equally unimpeachable.

Somehow, she deduced, she must have erred. When her stomach pains first began she blamed an apple, then a too-big slice of chocolate cake she had eaten at a birthday party. Whatever the cause of her discomfort, she assumed that (1) it had to be something she ate, and (2) once she discovered what that was, she had only to stop eating it and the pain would go away. In her seventy-five-year-old innocence, my mother assumed what she had always assumed: that she was in control and that if she did the right thing (i.e., ate the right thing) everything would come out right and she would be healthy.

She didn't know that with cancer such rules don't apply. She didn't know that, with cancer, no rules apply.

When even after the abandonment of chocolate cake and apples, the stomach pains didn't stop, her internist suggested a visit to her gynecologist, but it turned out she didn't have one. My mother had never been to a gynecologist, and somehow I had not known that. "Women of my age don't . . ." began her feeble explanation, no more feeble than my own when I asked myself how I could have not known. I had no answer, save an unconscious discomfort with the subject, at least as far as my mother was concerned. In addition there was that other, still stupider reason, the one that goes, Cancer happens to other people, not to me, not to her. That I had already been proven wrong on one of those assumptions didn't seem to have had an effect. It had been six years since the lump in my left breast turned out to be malignant. My still unreconstructed, half-flat chest continually reminded me that this was no bad dream. But it seemed like one anyway. After surgery, I found out my lymph nodes were clear, indicating no spread, which also meant no chemotherapy or radiation. So I never suffered—except in the head—and as a result of that, I suppose, it never seemed entirely real to me that I had had cancer. I *know* it didn't seem real to my mother. After a couple of years she allowed as how she had always thought the diagnosis had been a mistake.

Her internist recommended one Dr. Burns, a gynecologist and surgeon and a reputed heavy in the field of gynecological cancer. Humbled now by the stubbornness of the pain, she made an appointment with Dr. Burns. I went along.

We sat together in the brightly lit waiting room and turned the pages of *McCalls* and *Good Housekeeping*, then swapped when the wait turned into a half hour. When it got to be an hour, I moved on to the *Ladies' Home Journal* but abandoned it halfway into a tricky fruit pie recipe I knew I'd never make. Besides, I could see my mother wanted to talk. So we talked—not about what was on our minds, but about what color shoes would work with the jade green dress she planned to wear at my cousin's anniversary party a week from then.

The decision we finally came to (beige) turned out to be academic because the day before the party she was admitted to a hospital for the surgical removal of her ovaries and uterus and Fallopian tubes—the complete hysterectomy that Dr. Burns said she should have, and right away.

We gathered in the waiting room at the end of the tenth floor. My mother's younger sister, Shany, and I arrived first, then my husband, Ed, who came up on the subway as soon as he had finished teaching his math class at New York University, and finally Elaine, my cousin who had herself been sick with arthritis and whom I had told not to come. "Don't be silly," she said flatly. And I shut up because Elaine, who is a small person with the same mix of soft heart and hard head as my mother, had become my mother's chosen other daughter in recent years, and I knew she couldn't not be there any more than I.

In one way or another we were all four my mother's children. She had other "children," too, who probably would have been there had we let them know in time. My mother had never wanted me to be her only child—it had just turned out that way—and since she had no taste for deprivation, rather than do without she made children out of people who were not. They in turn were willing to be her children because, where was the harm? She loved them heartily and made them—us—feel what larger-than-life mothers always make people feel: that notwithstanding our age, she knew more, knew best, and always would.

Shany, born six years after my mother, had been my mother's child for as long as they both could remember. Into their seventies my mother told Shany what to wear, what to eat, and what to do. Not that Shany always obeyed. Especially in recent years, since her husband had died, then her daughter (of cancer at age forty-seven), Shany chain-smoked and ate crap and didn't care if she herself lived or died, and my mother couldn't seem to change *that*. Still, my mother scolded her, and Shany took the scoldings and bought the dresses my mother told her to buy and maybe even smoked fewer cigarettes each day than she otherwise would have.

Elaine, the fifty-five-year-old daughter of my mother's long-deceased sister Sarah, shoved her arthritis problems aside whenever she could (like both of our mothers, she took festivities as seriously as sickness) and had long been my mother's deputy planner of birthday parties, living rooms, and on occasion whole lives of other family members.

My husband Ed became my mother's child shortly

after we married, by which time she had absorbed what a peach he is. On the one hand, no one was good enough for her baby; on the other hand, she knew damn well he was and she couldn't get over our good fortune.

I say "our" because my mother did experience my good fortune as hers, and as neurotic and creepy as that may sound, it didn't feel that way. By that time in my life my mother and I held the same definition of good fortune—a good man like Ed and a good work life and good health—with some disagreement on the order. And it didn't bother me to have her join in the celebration of my good fortune, as it might have when I was younger. In fact I liked it. I liked that she saw in Ed what I saw—his big, silent sweetness; his brain; and, notwithstanding his brain, his lack of pomposity.

"Don't say 'son-in-law,' " she'd scold an innocent caller who had asked after him. "He is my son. I know his mother, may she rest in peace, would understand and forgive me for saying that. You can't love someone as much as I love my Ed and call him a son-in-law."

My mother's style wasn't for everyone. I know that. There are sons-in-law who might have recoiled from this assault of love, this avalanche of approval and affection. A midwestern WASP by birth and personality, my husband, I know, had neither seen nor experienced anything like it. His parents had loved him, but in Champaign, Illinois, "Good job, son" was about it for praise. At first he was stunned. Then he got used to it. And finally we'd get home at the end of the day and push the playback button on the answering machine and my mother's voice would chirp, "Hello-the-most-wonderful-children-any-mother-could-possibly-have! . . ." and five minutes later I'd have begun dinner and my mother would still be talking and Ed would have pulled a chair up to the machine and he'd have on his face a look of such interest and delight that one would think he was tuned in to a favorite radio program. In no time the reserved mathematician and his round, Jewish mother-in-law—the top of whose head came up to his tie—loved each other, in dissimilar styles but with equal ferocity.

So there in the hospital waiting room we sat, we children of my mother—Ed, Shany, Elaine, and me—and inhaled the stale smoke of the room's previous sitters and looked at without seeing the travel posters, and waited for Dr. Burns to appear and use the word *benign*. But when Dr. Burns finally came, he used the word *malignant* and also the word *metastasis*, and my hand flew to my mouth and Shany gasped and Elaine and Ed froze, and the surgeon had left the room and turned the corner before any of us thought to ask how long she had.

2
chapter

A telephone. I had to find a telephone. There were people I had promised to call. Shany would take care of family. Their brother, older, healthy and living up in Scarsdale, headed her list. Alvin headed mine.

Alvin was not one of my mother's children. He was in a special category, that of (for want of a better word) boyfriend. My mother had made him promise not to come to the hospital. In turn, he had made me promise to call him as soon as I knew anything, which I would have done anyway.

There were two phones in the corridor outside the waiting room, both in use. I planted myself between the two callers. One, a nattily dressed man in a dark suit, spoke softly into the receiver as if he thought it might break. The other, an overweight, dark woman, her blouse pulled out in back, spoke rapidly in a language I didn't recognize. She kept laughing and moving her feet around in a little dance as if she had to go to the bathroom. Suddenly she switched to English and in so doing, said everything twice. "Eight pounds, eight pounds!" she shouted into the receiver. "Yes, yes! Fine! Fine!"

It occurred to me now where I was—the gynecology floor. Birth happens here, I thought, as well as ovarian cancer. And all of those D&Cs in between. The thought of babies made my eyes fill. I felt jealous of the woman in front of me. I wanted to be one of the happy, excited people reporting a birth, not who I was, not reporting what I was reporting. The woman finished her call, dropped her handbag, bent down to pick it up. Still laughing, she looked up. "Esyuse me, esyuse me," she said, her blouse hanging all the way out now, and rushed down the hallway. I turned from her toward the telephone and dialed Alvin's number.

"It's malignant."

Silence. "How bad?"

"I don't know."

"Will you call me when you know?"

"Of course I will."

I hung up and stood there for a second with my hand still on the receiver. Is this real? It didn't feel real. But how does real feel? Someone else wanted to use the phone. I moved away, pushing my wallet back into my shoulder bag. Telling Alvin made it seem definite, but definite didn't seem real either. Nothing had changed. We just had a piece of information. Yet the piece of information changed everything.

* * *

Once she hit seventy, even before she had cancer, my mother used to say she was ready to die any time. After my father died she said it a lot. Then she met Alvin and she said it less. The whole business with Alvin was—and still is—a mystery to me. The first mystery is, with the shortage of unattached, sane, heterosexual men in the world and the abundance of women, how she got him. These do not, I know, sound like the kind words of a loving daughter. But the cold truth is that my mother was not beautiful or rich or any of the other things that one expects men to want. My mother had a sweet, oval face, lovely pale skin, and remarkably large, deep-set black eyes, and to me she was adorable, but I know to anyone else she probably looked like a garden-variety short, plump, occasionally over-rouged Jewish lady.

When I'd say that to Ed, he'd get huffy and point out my mother's other qualities and how men care about those things too. Sure, sure. But Alvin was and is, objectively speaking, a catch. He's refined and attractive. In spite of his short stature he has a regal way about him; it has something to do with how his head sits high on his neck, as if he's surveying his land (not that he has any). Alvin has, moreover, an enchanting sense of humor. He specializes in small, delicious witticisms which my mother always missed. This seemed to bother him not at all. In fact, he seemed to enjoy the way she never got his jokes. At the punchline he'd laugh, himself, and we'd laugh, too, and my mother would smile, enjoying the merriment but not exactly getting the joke. Alvin would take her hand then and give it a squeeze, just in case she felt left out, though I don't think she did.

Afterwards, if we were in a restaurant, he'd gently take her arm—"This way, Ida," he'd say—and guide her away from the wrong door toward which her hopeless sense of direction had inevitably led her. Perhaps because I had never seen anyone treat my mother that way—not even my father, who was far more protected by her than protective of her—it struck me as the sweetest thing I ever saw. I'd walk behind them with my arm in Ed's and poke him in the ribs, and he'd tell me to cut it out because he knew I was on the verge of clucking out loud.

My mother was older than Alvin by about seven years, a fact which she always believed she had kept from him. My hunch is that Alvin knew but didn't let on because he knew she didn't want him to know. That would have been like him.

During the eight years of their friendship (or whatever it was) they spoke on the phone every day—sometimes twice, my mother told me—and they had a standing date for dinner every Thursday night. Why Thursday I don't know. After dinner, as I understand what little I understand, Alvin would go back to her apartment and she would give him one of her atrocious baked apples and a cup of decaffeinated coffee (she'd have set out the two cups and saucers and creamer and small embroidered napkins on the table Thursday morning, as she'd have selected and pressed and laid out on her sofa the dress she planned to wear), and at around ten-thirty or so he would go home.

I think.

She called me on the phone one morning after their second or third date and asked me to meet her in the Schrafft's restaurant on Fifty-seventh Street and Third Avenue, one of a chain of tearooms, most of which are gone now. Schrafft's was staffed predominantly by Irish waitresses of good character who wore hair nets and served the kind of plain food that passed my mother's muster. "None of those mystery dishes here," she said more than once. Everything my mother thought worth saying she said more than once.

For as long as we both lived in New York, whenever my mother and I had anything weighty to discuss we'd meet at Schrafft's. There was something about the hair nets and the bud vases in the center of the shiny wood tables that made us both feel safe from whatever stormy revelation one or the other of us was about to unload. My mother always got there first. By the time I'd arrive, she would have angled for—and gotten—a table near the window. Her menu would be face down, since she would have already made her decision about what to order: tomato surprise, which, since she always ordered the same thing, was nothing of the kind. I'd kiss her on the cheek and sit down and pull off my coat, feeling late. I wasn't late; it's just that she had the annoying habit of always being early. Then I'd order another tomato surprise or whatever else guaranteed safety from a lecture on nutrition.

Our last major Schrafft's colloquy before the Alvin conference had occurred two years earlier, in May. In the interim many minor meetings had been held, but '75 was the big one. I shoved my scarf in the sleeve of my coat and sat down across the table from my mother and thought how different she had looked on that day. No doubt I had looked different too. On that day my mother was the wondering, the expectant one, the one poised to receive information from me, the agitated giver. She had looked remarkably calm, as if she trusted me. As if, whatever small bomb I might be planning to place on the table between us, she had come prepared to sit still during its explosion with her hat on and her purse in her lap and say to herself, "It's only a little explosion. The bud vase can be replaced." Which is what she did. In fact she did one better.

I hadn't even waited for the stuffed tomato before, in a rush of verbs, I told her that, having had my mastectomy just five weeks earlier, I now planned to leave my husband, run off with another man to live in another city, quit my job, and write a book about what it was like to have breast cancer. I felt pretty sure that no part of this agenda would shock her totally. She had known that my marriage had been faltering, that another man was hovering, that the surgery had made me a little crazy, and that whenever I got a little crazy I wrote about it. So I didn't think she'd faint. But I did, I suppose, expect something trite and parental: "Well (pause), I hope you know what you're doing." That sort of thing. Instead, with no perceptible change of facial expression, she looked down at her doily placemat, looked back up at me, tried—and failed—not to crack a small smile, sighed, and said, "You're not a *boring* daughter."

Had my mother been a Noel Coward type, I suppose I would have been less moved by her retort. But my mother was most assuredly not a Noel Coward type; nor would she ever be. She was just a mother who had, over the years, relaxed a little—relaxed far more than I ever expected her to. And although I knew the management of Schrafft's stood foursquare against any exhibit on the premises of physical demonstrativeness, I rose from my chair on that occasion and hugged my mother hard enough to topple the navy bowler from her head even though she had secured it in front, as she always did, with a pearl hatpin.

Most Schrafft's meetings, major or minor, were me talking, her listening—well, her *reacting*. My mother was never one to just sit there. Mostly I recited bulletins on my life, giving her the latest on new jobs, new dresses, old friends—not usually about new men. That, until I married, was a subject too touchy for Schrafft's.

But look at us now! For on this day not only did we talk in Schrafft's about a new man, but about *her* new man! Of course, thanks to my mother's special way of approaching a subject, I didn't know at first what she was talking about.

"Are you sure it's all right?" she said. My mother rarely began her sentences, as most people do, at the beginning of a paragraph. Her *its* were always unfathomable.

"Am I sure what's all right?"

"I don't want to do anything to embarrass my daughter." That's something else she did—talk to you about yourself in the third person. Probably the word *my* played a role; she particularly liked saying the word with me attached. There was a time when all of this made me wild. It still made me a little wild, but mostly it amused me—all the more after Ed came along and I had a husband to share the amusement.

"Mother," I said leaning back, "how could you possibly embarrass me?"

"By seeing a man I don't plan to marry." So *that's* what this is about. "Because all you have to do is say one word and—"

"Mother, for heaven's sake, it's not 1900. But by the way, why don't you want to get married?"

"You see! I'm embarrassing you!"

"Stop it! You are not embarrassing me. I'm just curious. People your age do get married, you know."

"Alvin is a wonderful friend. What do I need marriage for? I was married to your father for forty-three years. It was a wonderful marriage. I don't need to do it again."

Truthfully, I don't think Alvin wanted to get married

again either. He, too, had been widowed and had worked out some kind of agreeable single life for himself. Perhaps that was part of his attraction to my mother. So too, probably, was the fact that my mother didn't have dollar signs in her eyes. It's not that she didn't like money, but she kept her liking of money separate from how she felt about people who did or didn't have it.

My mother had another quality that must have lured Alvin, as it lured all of those people who became her "children." Probably it's the most alluring quality she had or, for that matter, anyone can have—why else do politicians and salesmen always pretend to have it?—my mother was truly interested in and engrossed by other people—what they were and what they thought and what they said. She was a world-class listener. And as a result, people talked to my mother, and I mean talked. Family talked, friends talked, even strangers at bus stops talked.

I know about the bus stop people because my mother would tell me about them afterwards. "I was waiting for the number five—you know how slow the number five is, if you miss it, it's a half hour before another comes along—anyway, I met this woman—very pretty, she looks a little like your cousin Anita but blond—and she told me the saddest story about her son's wife. They were living in San something—Antonio? Where is that, Texas? And they bought a house and . . ."

It's not, obviously, that my mother didn't talk herself. She talked plenty, especially about me. Then, after I married, about us. She exerted some self-control when we were around, but as soon as our backs were turned, I know she bored the pants off everyone whose acquaintance she made, no matter now briefly, in the city of New York. Even so, she gave more than equal time to the talker, and in addition to equal time she gave equal feelings. She listened with the same emotional oomph she had when she talked. I think most people don't do that. If they listen at all, the feelings valve is turned off. They listen because it's only fair and they have good manners. My mother didn't listen with her good manners. She listened with her good heart.

So no wonder people talked to her, people like me, people like Shany and Elaine, people like Alvin. Alvin talked to her a lot about the real estate business, in which she had tinkered herself. And in those conversations she was not a child who didn't get jokes, but a smart pal who got it all.

My mother was smart about other things, too, like life. Especially, she was smart enough to know that life had been good to her, so she went around feeling grateful. Her gratitude took the form of a kind of continual merriment, strange considering that the world she came from—Orthodox Jewish—had as its goals duty and accomplishment, not joy.

Of course my mother didn't get joyous until after she felt she had been adequately dutiful and accomplished. She had to feel deserving of the A-plus she gave herself in wifehood and motherhood (modesty never interfered with the high grades my mother gave herself or me) before she could let go and say whoopee. But once she said it, she said it loud and continually until the end of her life.

New York made a difference too. She and my father moved to an apartment there in the early seventies. My mother thrived in the city. She had never driven a car, so in the suburbs she had always had to rely on other people, mainly my father, to transport her. That didn't work very well for either of them. Dependence made my mother cranky, and occasionally she took it out on him.

But now in New York she could suddenly fly (which is to say, walk and take buses). She'd meet me for lunch in midtown, puffing happily, having spent the morning whipping through the small errands she created for herself, her cheeks flushed from the cold air. "Hello, sweetheart!" she'd call, waving a package when she saw me. "Wait'll you see what I found for (me, Shany, some niece, some nephew) on sale in Bloomingdale's!" The city made my mother young.

When my father died—I hate to say it because she would hate me to say it, but it's true—my mother got still younger. Not right away. First she grieved in the usual way and that went on for almost two years. Then she met Alvin, to whom—I don't like saying this either—she seemed to have much more to *say* then she did to my father. And soon I noticed, even apart from Alvin, that she had become a different sort of person than the eyes-on-the-road lady she had always been. I guess what happened to her is what happens to a lot of older people for whom things have turned out pretty well. They quit squeezing life as if it were a recalcitrant piece of fruit and start drinking the juice.

"I've become selfish," my mother took to saying with a wicked smile. And, thank goodness, she had. At last she had stopped living and breathing for my father and me. My father was dead. I was happily married to Ed, whom she had adored from the first. "My job is done," she was fond of saying. "So I can be selfish now."

Her idea of selfish was taking piano lessons. "I'm ashamed to tell you how much they cost!" she whispered, delighted with how much they cost. She also liked that her piano lessons proved me wrong. How could she spend fifteen dollars a lesson and be the tightwad (when it came to spending money on *herself*) I had always accused her of being?

And she didn't stop there. My mother—who had always eschewed everything that didn't have a purpose, usually connected with me—took up bridge. Wherever she went a notebook full of bidding strategies went with her. She studied them on supermarket check-out lines, on buses and on subways (I forebade her to take subways, but she took them anyway). Next, she joined the YWHA, where she folk danced twice a week and made as many friends as a child in a new school.

Meanwhile, I noticed, she dropped quite a few of the old friends and relatives, especially relatives, from her old duty-bound days. "All she does is complain!" she said of one. Then, after a pause, "All she *ever* did was complain! It's boring! Who needs it?" "Who needs it?" was her favorite new expression, delivered with the sass of a castinet click, as if she had always been the carefree fun-lover she had just become.

On occasion she wanted an audience for her new endeavors. "Now sit down," she commanded Ed and me one evening, pointing at the gold-colored sofa in her living room, preserved years longer than its normal life expectancy by slipcovers, antimacassars, and minimal use, now down at last to its original cover. "I'm your mother and it's a short piece." At which point she sat herself down at her still shiny Steinway spinet—where I had sat thirty-five years earlier with her standing behind me to make sure my back was straight—and demonstrated the results of her tenth lesson: a halting, but technically perfect rendition of Lara's theme from *Doctor Zhivago*. She struck the last chord and turned around, flushed from performer's high. "What do you think?" she said. "Not bad for an old lady, huh?"

That same year my mother and her new friend from the Y, Rose (who had lived in Mexico, wrote poetry, and wore fringed shawls) decided to join a theatrical group which had some kind of vague, charitable purpose. I think they gave performances for underprivileged children, none of whom was in sight the Saturday afternoon I found myself in the audience of a darkened theater somewhere near the East River, watching my mother throw herself into the role of the wicked stepmother in Hansel and Gretel.

She cheated, of course. She wore a dress that was much too nice, and her makeup looked as if Elizabeth Arden herself had risen from the grave to apply it. She also overacted, especially in the scene when the stepmother sends the children out into the woods. She made too many mean faces. But afterwards I complimented her extravagantly, just as she had complimented me extravagantly when I played Miss America with, as I recall, far less abandon in my sixth grade pageant, circa 1947.

But with all of that, even in these, her most carefree years, my mother remained within some of the boundaries of her past. As befitting a widow approaching seventy—even long before she became sick—she made the proper preparations for her death. This she did without a trace of martyrdom or even lugubriousness, but in a matter-of-fact way, as if any decent person would do the same.

No, that's not right. That sounds as if she were performing a duty, whereas my mother took a lot of pleasure and pride in these plans. She was proud that she was able to leave me money, even though I didn't need it and scolded her when she brought it up; proud, too, that she had taken certain steps so that her death wouldn't inconvenience Ed or me. She had selected and paid for a burial plot, handed us an extra key to her safe-deposit box so that we would have immediate access to it, saw to it that her bank accounts were in trusts for me, and bought bearer bonds only.

Not that she looked forward to the end. As she made these provisions, she tried not to think about what they meant. She didn't *want* to think about dying. But she admitted this only occasionally, as if there were something naughty about not wanting to die. During her first heart-to-heart with my husband, shortly after we announced our wedding plans, she told him how for two years after my father died she couldn't wait to "join him." "But then," she said with what my husband read as a guilty smile, "I found out I wasn't in such a hurry after all!"

Sometimes my mother's cheer was annoying—the way she'd insist on pointing out the bright side of everything, even when whatever it was didn't have one, like my first marriage. And she was always saying things that would have been better stitched on pillows: "Sometimes mistakes aren't mistakes; they're lessons!" *Can* it, Mother, I wanted to say and occasionally did. But she couldn't and I knew it. And when I looked around and saw other people's mothers ceaselessly criticizing their children and heard their the-world-owes-me-and-it-hasn't-paid-and-it-never-will blues, and then I got home from the office, aching tired, and turned on my answering machine to hear one of my mother's two- to five-minute warbles ("Hello, my darlings! This is the luckiest mother in the world speaking! . . ."), it was hard to feel abused.

And she asked so little of us! Too little. If we called, fine; if we didn't, fine. She was just all the gladder to hear from us when we did call. And we did call, not because we knew we should, but because we wanted to, because in her extremely special way she cheered us and amused us and enlightened us and of course praised us and so plainly and abundantly loved us as we loved her that . . .

Is this true? I wonder, am I doing what people do when someone they love has died? Are my remembrances of her gauzed? Am I making her out to be more, better, sweeter, than she was? It's hard to know. I loved her so much I felt it and can still feel it in the marrow of my bones, and as she got sicker, the love got weighty and painful—and it grew. Even the parts of her that were irritating seemed adorable and I started missing them even before she was gone. And as the weight and pain grew, I wanted to shake it. I tried. I took walks around the city and looked in shop windows and made myself think of other things, but I couldn't shake it. And sometimes I still can't.

3

chapter

Altogether, Dr. Burns said, she'd have eight chemotherapy treatments, one a month, and she would receive them all intravenously in the hospital. She'd get the first treatment, he said, before she went home. Pain from the tumor had been replaced by pain from the surgery, but each day brought a slight improvement. And on the eighth day after surgery, when they thought she could take it, a nurse wheeled the IV stand back in and the first treatment began.

"It's nothing," my mother said to me an hour after the resident stuck a needle into the vein on the back of her left hand. "I don't feel a thing. Honestly, sweetheart."

I heard the words and I knew the sound. It was the sound of my mother mothering me. Even now.

"You know," she said, turning her head on the pillow and looking over at me with her big, sweet, black eyes, "sometimes the fear is worse than the reality."

I knew that sound too. That was the sound of my mother making an embroidered pillow out of everything. I looked down and pressed my lips together so that she wouldn't see I had begun to cry.

"When I heard chemotherapy," she went on, "I thought, my God, I'll be nauseous, I'll be bald." She reached over and took my hand. "Do you know what Dr. Burns said?" I shook my head no. "He said if my hair falls out it'll grow back right away. And you know what else he said? He said it might even grow back bright red. Isn't that funny? Look at you. You have circles under your eyes. Go home. I'm fine."

I'm fine.

It's just as well they don't tell you what's in store. Because once you know, you get sick thinking about it. In the months that followed she'd often be nauseated even before the IV went in.

Chemotherapy isn't always the descent into hell it came to be for my mother. When Ed's mother got cancer, she breezed through hers. The word *chemotherapy* means drugs, and what sort of drugs they use depends on the kind of cancer cells they're trying to kill. Some drugs are less toxic than others. Some bodies react to them less adversely than others. Some patients enter a doctor's office, take a pill, go home, and maybe they don't attend a dinner dance that evening; but neither do they spend the next eight hours with their heads hung over a toilet bowl.

Not that my mother ever made it to the toilet. She'd vomit into those handy plastic receptacles—crescent-shaped like salad plates—they give you in stacks in the hospital.

She needed to go to the hospital for chemotherapy because the kind she got, cisplatin and Adriamycin, cannot be absorbed orally and therefore had to be administered intravenously. Each treatment spanned a weekend. On Friday afternoon I'd walk over to her apartment on East Fifty-fourth Street, across town from mine, and take her to the hospital in a taxi—when we could find one. As the weather got warm and people began going off for weekends in the country, finding an empty taxi on Friday afternoon got to be like a sporting event, one which my mother and I regularly lost. Young East Siders with natty luggage and long tanned arms outran and outwaved us on Third Avenue. Each time I got beat, I'd sweat uselessly and look back at my mother standing where I had told her to wait on the sidewalk, looking sad and small in a nice dress, holding her pocketbook like a child with a lunch pail, wearing the turban she had to wear now that her hair was gone.

I knew losing her hair was harder for her than she let on. She had such beautiful hair—thick and black and shiny, with only a few strands of gray at the temples. My mother had always been vain about her hair. She liked to tell about hairdressers and women friends who assumed she dyed it and how surprised they were to find out that she didn't.

When her hair didn't fall out right away, she began to think it might not. Then after the third treatment it started. "Look," she said to me in a low voice in her apartment one day, holding her hairbrush out for me to see. It was so matted with hair I almost couldn't see the brush. Then she pointed at her pillow, covered with black strands. "It's kind of messy," she said, trying to smile. After that she kept her head covered all the time. When she went outside, she wore turbans and only occasionally a wig, because she thought it *looked* like a wig (it did). At home she covered her head with a little, white, hair net sort of cap that made her look like a child in a bedtime story.

Like a child. I've said that twice now. The sickness did that to her. Moreover, she became a particular kind of child—quiet, docile, obedient, especially with her doctors and most especially in the hospital. I think she felt like a prisoner there, as though the medical staff were guards — and torturers—and if she were good maybe they'd torture her less. Even with the administrative people she was "good." Each Friday we waited in the hospital's admitting area for at least an hour because she insisted on being there exactly when they told her to be.

"Mother," I'd say to her on the phone on Friday morning, "why don't I come by a little later this time, say about three."

"But they told me two o'clock."

"I know, but remember what happened last time? We sat there until four."

"I know but . . ."

"There's no point," I'd say.

"Well, they must have a reason."

"Sure they have a reason," I'd snap at her and immediately hate myself. "That way it's easier for them. They can have you hanging around until the exact moment they want you. *They* don't care how lousy you feel."

In truth, I wasn't being fair. They were pretty nice at the admissions desk and didn't mind when we came later. And if I said Mother felt rotten, they usually succeeded in getting her into a room right away.

Nor was I fair—or particularly nice—to the elderly German volunteer who used to escort her to her room.

"Vait a minnit," she'd say, squinting up at us. "You look vamiliar. You bin here bevore?"

"About four thousand times," I'd say, not sweetly, hoisting my mother's overnight bag over my shoulder and moving ahead of both of them toward the elevator.

"Ach zo, I zee you know the vay."

"Right," I called back, as my mother smiled at her and said pleasant things about the warm weather.

All I was doing—I didn't realize it then, of course—was what people often do when they've been hit and there's nobody to hit back. Hit back anyway. The people at the hospital were as good targets as anyone, and there were occasions when they deserved to be hit back. But mostly they were okay. It was cancer that wasn't okay—cancer, and what they did to try to make it go away.

4

chapter

My mother surprised me. I wouldn't have guessed how much she wanted to live. I would have thought she'd have picked death over torture, but here she was, back on the starting line for the fourth weekend of chemotherapy (four more to go), sick and weak and bald and, by now, stripped of illusion about what lay ahead. But she didn't flinch and, as far as I knew, she didn't even consider quitting.

The fourth Friday was a steamy, fetid twenty-first of August. People on the street looked drugged from the heat. Eyes stared ahead but didn't seem focused. Mouths hung open as if the hinges that held them together were broken. Old people looked faint; young people looked angry. Crossing the avenues on the way over to my mother's apartment, I made wide circles at each corner because the litter baskets had overflowed and food and flies and soft drink cans had spilled onto the sidewalks and into the gutter. Altogether, it was the kind of day in New York that in itself is a punishment, the kind of Friday in New York when if you have five dollars, you get out.

There were no empty taxis, none, and my mother's nausea had already begun. I heard it in her voice when we spoke on the phone that morning. "Are you okay?" I asked.

"Yes . . . I'm okay." That's what she always said. I only knew how sick she was by the length of the pause.

When I got to her apartment she was still getting dressed. I didn't even ask her how she felt. I didn't need to. She moved as if she were underwater, and she spoke almost not at all. The elevator was slow in coming, like everything else that day. She waited with her head down, her eyes fixed on the unpatterned carpet. She looked up when she got outside. The heat seemed to startle her. I took her arm and slowly, silently, we made our way up the street. An elderly man selling fruit on the corner of Third Avenue let her sit on one of his empty crates while I stepped off the curb and began waving my arm for a taxi. After ten minutes I noticed a bus crawling up the avenue.

"What do you think?" I called to her, motioning toward the bus. "Sure," she said, and we got on.

I spotted a seat toward the back and was so grateful, it was a few minutes before I realized the air-conditioning was broken. People had opened the windows, but the thick, hot breeze changed nothing for the better. My mother, her face gray, sat erect throughout the ride. With one hand she held tight the pole next to her. With the other she held a handkerchief over her mouth.

She felt a little better—or so she said—walking the few blocks from the bus stop to the hospital. But when we arrived, a bony, tight-lipped woman I had never seen before at the admissions desk gave me a "You'll just have to wait" without looking up from her writing. When I explained in my most hushed, refined voice that my mother felt awful, she continued not to look up and, once again, gave me her recorded announcement. At that moment I had an impulse which gave me a better understanding of homicide than I had had before, to grab the pencil out of her hand and stab her through the heart. Instead, I went back to where I had left my mother sitting in the waiting area and took her hand and told her the room would be ready soon.

"Ida Rol-lin." When that witch called my mother's name only ten minutes later, I thanked her and felt a rush of guilt about my fantasy. When she still didn't look up, the guilt vanished like a shadow. No matter, I thought, with the single-minded relief of one who has just gone from standby to passenger. Besides, another, more choice target for my crankiness was fast approaching. The little German lady in her robin's egg blue volunteer smock waddled up to us and reached for my mother's overnight bag. She stopped, looked up, and squinted.

"You bin here bevore?"

Once in the room on the now hatefully familiar tenth floor, my mother sat slumped on the edge of the bed. As I helped her undress I noticed, with relief, that the other bed in the room was unoccupied. The past few times when she felt all right on Friday night, my mother had made fast friends with her roommates. Generally, they seemed good for her, this succession of ladies with gynecological and God knows what other kinds of trouble (by Saturday night my mother knew), but this time, I thought, better without.

"Thank you, sweetheart," she said in her new, beaten voice, raising her arm like a good child so that I could pull off her blouse. She still took care about how she dressed to go to the hospital, although her clothes were so big for her now, they looked as if they belonged to somebody else. She wore makeup too—a little foundation, rouge, lipstick. My Aunt Shany, who sometimes took my mother to the hospital instead of me and always sat with her for hours during the chemotherapy weekends, had her own theory about the makeup. In our daily phone conversations during the course of my mother's illness, Shany would ask about what her sister had on her face in trying to assess how sick or well she was.

My mother, as Shany knew, didn't merely wear makeup; she *believed* in it. She spent a good portion of her life trying to get the women she loved most—especially Shany and me—to wear more. To my mother, makeup—judiciously applied of course—was an act of friendliness to oneself, a gesture of love and respect toward one's face. Shany held the theory, therefore, that as long as her sister Ida kept wearing makeup, she still must be herself. And if she were still herself, there was still hope. Hope for what, I wondered—not out loud—that cream rouge could cure cancer?

When the aide came in with her chart I told her I'd answer the questions for my mother. By now I had learned a few ropes in the hospital and one of them was to recite "two" to all questions from the lady with the chart. "Nightgowns?" "Two." "Stockings?" "Two." She looked up at me and we had our first eye contact. This had to mean she was confused about something. Confusion was the only motive I knew for eye contact from floor aides.

"Two stockings or two pairs?" "Two pairs," I said. Even with the interruption, the quiz took half the time it would have with the patient answering. My mother labored over the questions as though they were college boards.

She lay in the bed now, on her back with her eyes closed. She shivered a little. As usual, the air-conditioning had overchilled the room. I pulled the blanket up under her chin. "How about another blanket?" I asked her. She nodded. Right at that moment another aide walked in and filled the water pitcher. "Got another blanket?" I said in what I thought was a pleasant tone of voice. She didn't answer.

"Do you have another blanket?" I said again.

"I heard you," she said, not breaking stride. "When I have time I'll get you one." She walked out. Okay, black girl, so you think I'm a white princess and you hate me. Fine, but don't take it out on my mother, okay? I yanked a blanket off the other bed.

Next arrival, the sleep-deprived intern with *his* quiz: "When did you first feel sick, Mrs. Rollin? . . . Yes? And then what happened?" I never understood why they made her recite the history of her disease each time. It must have been written down somewhere. Somewhere, yes, but not conveniently located in front of their noses the way the patient was.

This intern was of the thin, hairy, pale, rabbinical student variety with a manner so gentle and a voice so low I could hardly hear him. Neither could my mother. "Excuse me?" she kept saying to every question he asked. Then he'd repeat it, no louder except for the first syllable of the first word. She stared at his face, trying to read his lips, concentrating hard and answering each question fully, the way she did with the chart lady.

It surprised me to hear her ask a question herself. "Doctor," she began, her voice breaking the way it always did when she was tired or sick or both, "lately I've started to feel nauseous before I come to the hospital, sometimes the night before. Like last night." She smiled almost apologetically. "Why does that happen? Is there something I can take?"

As my mother spoke, the intern nodded his head. "It's probably emotional," he murmured. "You anticipate what's going to happen and you get sick before it happens. It's very normal."

My mother smiled again and nodded. She seemed satisfied with his explanation, as if hearing the word "normal" took her off the hook. As if she had been feeling she must be crazy or bad to get sick before she was supposed to. "Thank you, Doctor," she said and closed her eyes again, all three of us having forgotten her other question—how to make it stop. Or maybe we didn't forget. Maybe, by now, we had all absorbed the fact that although medical science had figured out how to stop polio, the clap, and pregnancy, it hadn't yet figured out how to stop or even significantly slow down the nausea associated with chemotherapy.

Marijuana worked for some people, but you couldn't bring it into the hospital. The doctors said it wouldn't help my mother anyway because of the particular kinds of drugs she took. Besides, she had never smoked any kind of cigarette. How can you smoke dope if you've never smoked a Marlboro?

I looked at her. Her face had some color. Today's sickness seemed to have passed. Not that today was the problem. The problem, as we all knew, was tomorrow, when the chemotherapy would begin.

I knew it was a waste of time to ask the doctor about medication for tomorrow, but I followed him out the door and asked him anyway. I had been doing that sort of thing a lot lately, asking questions to which I knew there were either no answers or unsatisfactory ones.

I got the answer I expected. "Well, we'll give her Compazine."

"I know, but Compazine doesn't seem to help."

"Yeah." The intern shook his hairy head. "Cisplatin's rough. Maybe we could increase the dose of Compazine. I'll speak to the resident."

"Thanks," I said. He kept standing there as if he didn't like his answer any more than I did. It touched me, the way he stood there. "Thanks for being so nice to my mother," I said.

He looked surprised. "Oh, that's okay." He blushed and bounded down the hallway, his hairy head preceding his body, which looked skinny even in his big, white medical coat. He needs a good night's sleep, I thought. If his mother saw him she'd be upset, and she'd be right. Then I smiled because I realized that, if my mother were herself, that's what she would have said.

Dr. Burns came by at six that evening. He always made rounds about this time with his entourage—at least one resident and sometimes two or three who followed him down the corridor and into the rooms like a sixth grade class on a field trip. Dr. Burns had, I had to admit, a stolid, no-necked, husky kind of good looks. His hair, though white, was thick as an English schoolboy's and fell into one eye in a way I would have thought charming, were it possible for me to connect, in any way, the word *charming* with Dr. Burns. He stood at the foot of my mother's bed, accompanied on this trip by only one resident, a subdued Indian who kept his head bowed and his arms crossed in front of him as if he were attending a religious ceremony.

"How're you doin', Ida?" said Dr. Burns.

My mother blinked. "Oh fine, Dr. Burns," said the good girl, knowing what Daddy wanted to hear. Then she got brave. "Actually, I haven't been feeling very well . . ."

"Well, we'll try to fix you up," the doctor boomed,

pulling the curtain shut around her bed to examine her. I walked outside the room and leaned against the wall. I wish I didn't hate Dr. Burns, I thought. I'm probably wrong to hate him. Mother adores him. She even thinks he adores her. She thinks of herself as his favorite child. Maybe she is, the way she smiles and coos in his presence, the way she reveres him. She is full of reports to me and Shany (Shany hates him too) of how other people revere him as well, of what a "big man" he is.

He's big all right—too big. Too big at least to be interested in boring things like nausea. The cancer seems to interest him but not, goddamnit, how she *feels*. And he never answers a question so that you understand. Even she admits that, but she accepts it as part of his bigness. "What did he say, Mother?" I'd ask her after an appointment. "Well," she'd answer with the beginnings of a smile, "you know Dr. Burns. He told me to go home and watch the game." "The *what?*" "The baseball game—or was it the football game—on television." "But what did he say about the pain in your side?" "Well, he wasn't too clear about that . . ."

I rubbed my eyes with my thumb and forefinger. I had one of those sharp little headaches right behind the eyeballs. Oh well, I thought, Dr. Burns is a surgeon. They're like that. They're technicians. And we have every reason to think that Dr. Burns is an especially fine technician. Maybe that's enough. Maybe it's not fair to expect a fine technician to be a human being. It isn't as if he's mean. He's just remote. Maybe he has to be remote to protect himself. That's reasonable, isn't it? I wished someone of authority would drop through the ceiling and tell me it was reasonable. I wanted to think it was.

I walked down the corridor to the waiting room and fell into one of the plastic armchairs. *Visit Portugal* commanded a poster on the opposite wall. It could be my fault, I thought, not for the first time. Maybe I put him off in some way. Whenever I speak to him—and I try not to if I can help it—he makes me feel stupid and intrusive. But possibly it's me, something I do that makes him act that way. Or maybe I exaggerate his coldness—or whatever it is. I can't even quite put my finger on what he does that makes me feel so awful. Unless it's the way he doesn't look at me when I speak to him, but rather at the floor or over my head.

I flashed back suddenly to a moment I had had with him after my mother's hysterectomy. They had wheeled her into her room, moaning and writhing in pain. I knew she could hardly be expected to be comfortable after surgery, but I also knew there were drugs that were supposed to help. Then I found out they had discontinued painkilling drugs in the recovery room because her blood pressure had gone down. Later, however, I had the impression from the resident that the danger had not been great and that he and the hospital and probably all hospitals make it a policy to err on the side of safety. Patients don't die of agony, it turns out, even though they might want to. Nor will a patient's agony ever get a hospital staff member into trouble; a patient's death might. All of which makes agony, however unbearable to the person who's feeling it, quite bearable to those *caring* for the person who's feeling it.

For this value system, I had the further impression, one is supposed to feel monumentally grateful, just as I was supposed to feel grateful to the private duty nurse I had hired the day of surgery who informed me that my mother's suffering, on a scale of one to ten, merely hit a three or so. "You can tell when they're in severe pain," she said pleasantly. "They clench their fists." She demonstrated by making a fist with her right hand. Then she looked down at my mother, whose face was contorted, but whose fist, though closed, was not clenched. "You see," she said with a knowing smile, "this patient isn't doing that."

Her lecture could not have provided the comfort intended, because the next thing I remember is tearing down the corridor in search of Dr. Burns in order to get him to do something. I found him at the nurses' station. When I told him what I wanted (admittedly without a trace of calm), he spoke not a word in return but rather turned away from me and toward the nurse, ordering her in hospitalese to give my mother another shot of whatever, which the nurse promptly did. So Dr. Burns came through at that moment, and what did it matter whether he came through warmly to me? Warmth we can all get somewhere else. Besides, my mother finds him warm. Or she wants to, therefore she does.

I leaned my wrists against the arms of the plastic chair, pushed myself up, and slowly walked back to her room. Dr. Burns and the resident were gone and, happily, in their place was my favorite Irish nurse, thrashing about in her customary bull-in-a-china-shop style. I truly loved Irish, although she took some getting used to. Her entrances, for example, were alarming. Such was the force of her stride she seemed in continual danger of overshooting the bed and going through the wall. And that voice. That voice could have awakened the comatose.

"How about another-r pillow, Mrs. Rollin? And how'r-r you dear-r," she said to me, continuing her stomp around the room, inspecting corners and drawers as if in search of subversives.

"I'd love another pillow," said my mother, smiling. "How did you guess?"

"Par-rt of the job dear-r, par-rt of the job. I'll be r-right back," which she was in an instant, not with one pillow but two.

"Isn't she cute?" whispered my mother to me after Irish had bounded out. "She lives with her sister. I don't think she's ever been married. Her sister used to be a nun. She—"

I bent over my mother to straighten her white cap, and kissed her on the forehead. "You're pretty cute yourself," I said, and she smiled.

I knew it would probably be her last smile until we got her out of there.

5

———————◆———————

By the time I arrived at about eleven Saturday morning, the IV bag hanging from the pole next to her bed was already half empty and she was dozing. Good, I thought. If only she'd stay asleep through the whole thing. Careful not to make a sound, I put down my newspaper and yogurt and eased myself into the chair at the foot of the bed.

"Hi, sweetheart."

"I woke you."

"No, you didn't. I've been sleeping on and off all morning."

Her words slurred slightly. That would be the Thorazine, which they would have given her by now. Until my mother's illness I had thought of Thorazine as a tranquilizer used to sedate crazy people in state institutions. That's not wrong, but it has other uses as well, one of which is to dull the senses of cancer patients before blasts of chemotherapy. Thorazine made her sleepy all right—it even put her in a kind of stupor—but it didn't seem to make her any less sick. Compazine was supposed to do that. But it didn't.

Irish was off today. Her understudy bustled in to take temperature and blood pressure. She was a young, peppy little thing, a cheerleader in type, but without the frozen smile. I liked her. "Hi!" she said. "Hi!" said my mother and I in unison, as if in a return cheer.

Just then a sound came from the other side of the room and I noticed the curtain had been drawn around the bed. Someone must be in it. I jerked my thumb in its direction and in a stage whisper asked my mother who. She shrugged. "Some woman they brought in late. She was up all night."

I knew what that meant; it meant my mother was up all night too. I sighed. Well, maybe it's better if she's tired. Maybe it's going to be better this time, period.

There's a name for that. It's called wishful thinking. It has a reputation it deserves for not getting results.

"Why don't you try to go back to sleep," I said. She nodded and closed her eyes. I watched her, thinking as I did that I should eat my yogurt now. Eat it, the point was, before her vomiting started. But I didn't feel like eating it. Instead I sat, dumb, and stared at her eyelids, which were trembling. Perhaps she's having a dream, a nice (more wishful thinking) dream.

The day, at least, had brought one victory. Her brother, Louis, had wanted to come and I had talked him out of it. Why should he see this? I said to Shany and she agreed. It was bad enough, tenderhearted soul that he was, that he knew about it. Both my mother and Shany were tougher than he. I suspected they always had been, even though he was older, eighty now, the oldest living child of Rebecca and Solomon Silverman, who, along with hundreds of thousands of other Eastern European Jews, came to this country at the start of the twentieth century, to find a better life—and did.

The Silverman children were born between the years 1901 and 1912, the older two in Bialystok, Poland—one of those towns near the border that keep becoming a part of Russia—and the younger two in New York. Sarah came first, fat, giggly, flirty Sarah who had baby-sized teeth even after she grew up and who, in fact, never altogether grew up, although she married, of course, and had five children and a couple of grandchildren before she died of a stroke at fifty. Louis came next, kind and quiet as a boy and as a man, kind and quiet, his sisters thought, to a fault. "He never learned to fight," they sighed. "So he never got what he should."

In 1908, Ida became the Silvermans' first American-born child and because of this received a kind of perpetual deference and respect from her parents, for whom everything American had an ingrained gloriousness. Like her brother, Ida was serious and smart, but she lacked her brother's timidity—lacked, in fact, any timidity. The American-born child, her mother always thought, will make her way in the American world. "We don't have to worry about Ida," her parents said to each other in Yiddish.

The birth of the last child, Shany, came in the winter of 1912. Shany, the pretty, sweet, impulsive one. Bright too, but Shany didn't care about the attributes fate bestowed on her. What she cared about was her first cousin Louis, eight years her senior, who gave her an engagement ring when she was thirteen and whom she married at seventeen. Her mother cried, but only at first. After all, Louis was a good boy and her brother's son.

The Silvermans lived on the fourth floor of number 514 East 139th Street in the Bronx in a small, dark, boxy cluster of rooms, each one dimly lit by a gas fixture that hung from the center of the ceiling. When the lights flickered, Poppa knew it was time to deposit a quarter in the gas meter, a large box high up on the kitchen wall. Sometimes he'd lift baby Shany up and let her put the money in. "It's a bank," he'd tell her, and for years she thought it was.

The apartment's amenities were few: no heat save that which came from a coal stove in the kitchen, little natural light since only two of the rooms had windows, and of course no telephone. They did have an icebox, which caused occasional floods when Momma forgot to empty the tray underneath.

The apartment had two bedrooms. Momma and Poppa slept in one, the three girls occupied one big bed in the other, and Louis, who didn't sleep in a real bed until he married, slept on a cot in the parlor.

Louis's good nature made him first up each morning at six, when he'd shovel coal for the kitchen stove so that Poppa wouldn't have to do it. And since he had a job during the day and went to school at night, he was last to retire. He'd steal into the apartment late each night like a burglar, carefully open his parents' bedroom door, feel the top of his mother's head to make sure she hadn't left any hairpins in which might hurt her, tiptoe out, and crawl into his cot.

Every morning when he arose at seven, Poppa sat himself down to pray and study at the big dining table that occupied most of the dining room. This he did all morning. In the afternoon Poppa received his students—small

American boys with fallen socks—whom he taught Hebrew and prepared for their bar mitzvahs. In the evening,
after a dinner of flanken (boiled beef), boiled potatoes,
and applesauce—never salad, Poppa said salad was for
rabbits—he'd turn to the day's only entertainment, the
Jewish *Daily Forward*. Momma couldn't read, so when he
got to something good—usually from the Bintel Brief—
Poppa would read out loud. The Bintel Brief was a kind
of Yiddish Ann Landers which ran letters with operatic
themes written by women who came from Europe to join
their husbands only to find them Changed, e.g., in the
arms of some Reform Jewish lady from Brooklyn.

The family was poor, but they didn't know it because
everyone was poor. Of course some people were even
poorer and Momma's heart bled for them all, especially
those who were nearby, like Mrs. Binowsky, the widow
who lived in the apartment next door. Mrs. Binowsky
earned what little money she had as a dressmaker. So
whenever Mrs. Binowsky couldn't pay her rent, Momma
would order a dress for one of her girls. The hitch was
Mrs. Binowsky had terrible eyesight and she made mistakes when she sewed. As a result the Silverman girls had
awful-looking dresses. But they had a lot of them.

Of this the girls did not complain, at least not to their
mother. They had long since accepted the fact that their
mother was an emotional sponge, a soft touch, particularly when it came to emotions like grief, desperation,
fear, and panic. Charity seekers found their way to the
Silvermans' door like birds landing on a feeder. And no
bird ever flew away hungry. That was a rule of the house,
and not only because Momma said so. The religion said so
too; no matter how little you have, you give something.

Momma had a special weakness for orphans. If Momma
heard about an orphan who needed money, she gave even

before anyone asked. That was because Momma herself had been an orphan. Her mother had died in childbirth, her father two years later.

"If you had no parents, who took care of you, Momma?" the children used to ask.

"Everyone who was afraid of God," she'd say.

Momma and Poppa spoke no English. They didn't have to. Their world was their apartment and their block and the grocery on the corner and the synagogue and the family and the peddlers who came to the door, and everyone in that world spoke Yiddish. Still, they loved the sound of the English words, or at least Momma did. It thrilled Momma that her children spoke the English language. For her it was like going to a concert. She didn't understand the music, but what did it matter? She knew her children were fine musicians.

Momma did learn a few words—*yes, no, so-so* (which she liked saying with the appropriate accompanying gesture, a small rotation of her right hand), and her favorite, *surprise!*, always said with an exclamation point. No one remembered precisely when or why she developed her fondness for *surprise!*, but like a child with a big rubber ball, she threw it into the conversation at every opportunity. It got on everybody's nerves just a little bit. "No, Momma," the children would say in Yiddish. "You don't mean *surprise!* You mean *good* (or *that's nice*, or whatever). But Momma would shake her head and laugh. She liked *surprise!* better.

When Ida told her parents she wanted to go to college, Poppa said, "Why does she need college?" Nobody had a good answer, but she went anyway because Momma wanted her to. *Wanted* is putting it mildly. When Ida received her letter of acceptance from the Maxwell Training School for Teachers in Brooklyn—there was a Jewish quota and she might easily not have made it—Momma reached up (she stood only four feet ten inches) and took her daughter's head in both her hands as if it were a melon and gave her a big, smacking kiss on the forehead. If she could have done it without disgracing her husband, Momma would have hoisted the American flag and held her own celebration march down 139th Street.

Momma was no more thrilled than Ida herself, who had wanted to be a teacher for as long as anyone could remember. To say Ida loved children did not convey the intense feeling she had when confronted with any member of the human species under the age of ten. She was particularly taken with the children in her family. Happily, sister Sarah and her brood had moved next door. Of Sarah's children, Ida's favorite was the oldest boy, Pincus, who as a baby got passed by his mother to his aunt over the back fence like a basket of food. As he grew older, Pincus became a bit of a brat, but he remained Ida's little prince. She took him everywhere, even to her portrait photo session for her high school graduation. Once in the studio Pincus decided he wanted to be photographed too. As a result, Ida's portrait was the only one of her high school graduation class to include a fat-faced five-year-old boy in a sailor suit.

Predictably, the part of college Ida liked best was student teaching. She also liked psychology and English and excelled in them. Throughout her three years she had only one problem at Maxwell, but it was a serious one because it nearly prevented her from getting her diploma. In order to graduate from the Maxwell Training School for Teachers every student, with no exceptions, was required as part of her gymnasium class to execute at least one regulation somersault. Ida Silverman, try as she did—and she did try—could not do this.

Part of her difficulty, no doubt, was a lack of experience

with any kind of physical activity, especially an activity that required a reversal, however short-lived, of head and feet. Exercise played no role in the household of Solomon and Rebecca Silverman. Solomon held the belief that people who used their bodies did so for one reason—because they had no minds. Sports, in other words, were for the goyim.

In addition, the Silverman girls were not exactly sports naturals. They were, in fact, fat and clumsy. It's hard to roll over upside down if you're fat and clumsy; you get stuck on your neck or you fall over on your side, all of which happened to poor, earnest Ida. And the more it happened, the more desperate she got.

Fortunately, she was not alone. There was another fat girl, Sue, who couldn't make it either. So they'd practice together, mostly at Ida's house. Momma would help them drag the mattress from the bed in Ida's room into the parlor, where they'd drop it on the floor and then go at it. Momma tried to time these sessions so that Poppa would be at the synagogue. But on one or two occasions Poppa arrived home early, and standing stone still at the doorway he observed his daughter and her friend in their gymnasium bloomers, their faces flushed, their behinds in the air, rolling around on the mattress in the parlor. He would utter not one word. He'd just shake his head and, as quickly as possible, go into the dining room and pray.

They finally got the hang of it—first Ida, then Sue—and in 1929 they won their diplomas. Immediately, they set about looking for jobs as teachers. But there weren't any, and soon there wouldn't be any jobs of any kind. What skills Ida lacked as a tumbler, however, she made up for as both a quick study of reality and a fast talker. By September, just a few months after graduation, she landed a position in the personnel department of Beth Israel Hospital in Manhattan.

Momma thought that was wonderful. Momma thought everything her children did was wonderful. And to think a person could just like that, one, two, three, get a job and that person is your daughter and the job is at a nice Jewish hospital—that was really wonderful. What a country, said Momma. What a wonderful country.

The vomiting began right on schedule at two-thirty. The first hour she vomited every fifteen minutes, then every ten, then after three hours, every twenty, on into the evening. In between vomiting she dozed or sometimes she just lay there with her eyes closed. After the first couple of hours she no longer had enough strength to lift her own head and wipe her own mouth.

Every few hours the cheerleader pulled down the covers, rolled her over, and plunged a hypodermic needle filled with Compazine into her backside. I was wrong, the nurse told me, to think Compazine didn't help. I half smiled at her. "You mean without the Compazine it would be worse?" She nodded and, leaving me with that thought, sped down the hallway.

"Oh please," my mother moaned. I shot out of my chair. "Oh please," she moaned again. Her eyes were closed. She moved her head from side to side as if someone had her by the throat.

"Mother," I said, bending over her, "what can I get you? What can I do?"

Suddenly her eyes opened very wide and she turned them on me like headlights. "I'm so sick," she gasped, reaching for my hand as if she were about to fall. "I'm so sick."

I kissed her forehead, and felt her perspiration on my lips. "It'll stop soon," I lied. "It'll stop soon." Oh God, I thought, please let it be true. Please somebody make this end. Make this end. Please. She closed her eyes.

"I'll get you something cold for your head." I ran into the bathroom, let the water run cold, held a washcloth under it, wrung it out hard, and ran back and folded it across her forehead, all the while allowing myself to feel as if there were some point to this action, even though I knew there was no point to this action. With her eyes still closed, her hand moved up to adjust the wet cloth. Then, for a moment, she was still. Then she rolled her head from side to side as she had before and the cloth fell off. As I began to put it back on her forehead she shook her head no and pointed toward the plastic dish. I grabbed it and put it under her chin and she vomited. And because I didn't pick her head up in time, she gagged, then vomited again. What she vomited was green. I had seen it before. It was bile.

An interesting torture, this. You sit at your mother's bedside. Next to her on a steel pole hangs a plastic bottle filled with liquid. Each time you look up, the level of the liquid in the bottle has dropped. You know the reason for this. The reason is that the liquid is dripping into your mother's vein. You know this is good. You know the liquid is on its way to the cancer cells and that its mission is to destroy them. The liquid, therefore, is a friend, a most important friend. This your brain tells you. But this "friend" tortures your mother. This your eyes tell you. Somewhere between your brain and your eyes you feel these facts racing toward each other like two speeding cars. You almost want them to crash, because maybe the crash will wake you up and you will find your face in a pillow, your hair sticking to your face from sweat, and you will roll over knowing it was only—oh, sweet relief—a dream.

The aide returns from her break. Her name is Pearl. She is a small black woman, round as a puff pastry, with a sweet-sad, shy smile, a young girl's smile, although I guess her to be thirty-five, maybe more. Pearl has one child, a teenage daughter who she tells me is "a good girl," as if no more need be said; an absent husband (no more need be said about him either); and this rotten job which she says she likes "as long as the people is nice."

Pearl is wonderful with my mother. She is calm. She is efficient. She is gentle. And her body seems to house an internal alarm system set to go off seconds before my mother needs to throw up. The alarm system is a fine thing because it enables Pearl to get to my mother and hold her up, get the plastic dish under her chin and the tissues wadded up in her hand, all in time. As she performs these tasks, Pearl whispers to my mother. I can't hear the words, but I can hear the tone, which is tender, steady, immeasurably sweet. Without warning, my eyes fill up and I know it is not only the sight of my mother on the rack which moves me, but the rush of love I feel for this paid stranger, this black person in our employ who cradles my mother's hairless, white head in her bosom and murmurs to her as if she were her baby.

It is eight o'clock and my mother vomits again. I don't know why I look at the clock each time, as if there were something finite to this, something which can be counted, a numerical ending.

She no longer opens her eyes, although I don't think she is sleeping. I get up from my chair and walk past the other bed, now curtained, to the window. I know the afternoon has gone, but the darkness outside startles me. I put my forehead on the pane and look at the sky and the stars. It is a beautiful, indeed a faultless, summer evening.

6
chapter

Ed and I tore up to the hospital Sunday morning the way we always did because of the fear I always had that they'd have gone too far and killed her. In my head I knew that no such thing had happened, but my head wasn't in charge anymore.

Instead of dead we found her, as always, half dead, her shoulders rounded, her body slumped as if the bones had been removed, her lips and cheeks puffy from Thorazine so that the sounds coming out of her mouth only resembled words. She was too weak by far to walk. Yet she sat propped up in a chair, street clothes on, shoes included, hat a little crooked but secure and—yes, Aunt Shany—made up. On her lap she held the plastic vomiting dish as if it were a purse. I asked her, as I always did, if she wanted to stay in the hospital just a little while longer until she felt better and she said, as she always did, working her mouth to make the words come out, "Please, sweetheart, take me home," so of course we did.

We had permission to take the wheelchair outside, right up to the door of a taxi. Ed helped ease her into the back seat and then ran around and sat in front with the driver and tried to steer him around potholes. I stayed with my mother in the back and held her around the shoulders. The nurse on the floor had given us a stack of plastic dishes, but she needn't have. No matter how sick my mother felt, she never threw up in a taxi, not once. She was proud of that.

We didn't talk much on the way home. We never did. My mother sat as straight as she could, both hands holding the car seat as if to steady it. Her eyes were open, but I don't think she saw anything. When we got her home she threw up one more time. She did this quietly and matter-of-factly, sitting on a footstool which she kept in the bathroom and could easily pull over in front of the toilet. She kept the bathroom door closed and ordered Ed into the living room. I was allowed to wait outside the bathroom door, but she did not let me in until she was through. Then she pushed the door open and let me help her up and slowly walk her into her bedroom. I got her out of her clothes and into her nightgown and eased her under the bed covers, where she curled up on her side the way small children do on car seats and fell immediately and soundly asleep.

I tiptoed out (needlessly—she was out cold and would stay that way for a few hours at least, until the first layer of drugs wore off) and found Ed on the living-room sofa surrounded by the Sunday *Times*.

"She asleep?"

I nodded, pushed the book section out of the way and fell onto the other side of the sofa.

He looked at me. "How are you?"

"Fine," I said. "How are you?"

"Fine. This is a fascinating conversation."

I laughed. "How come you're such a card?"

He moved over next to me and kissed the side of my head. "How come you're such an easy laugh?"

I sighed. "How come it's such a shitty world?"

"It's not. Only sometimes it's shitty."

I let my head drop back on the sofa and stretched my legs straight out in front of me. It was a good time to read the paper, but I didn't feel like reading the paper. I didn't feel like moving any part of my body, not even my eyes, which had landed on the opposite wall where a framed photograph slowly came into focus. It was a wedding photo of Ed and me and our mothers, all wearing expressions of giddy joy (my mother and I, admittedly, giddier than the other two). My eyes slowly panned each face, left to right, like a movie camera: my mother, eyes wide, mouth slightly open, as if she's about to pop out of the picture; me, my hair mussed from all the hugging, smiling with more teeth than I knew I had; Ed, grinning, also with teeth; my mother-in-law, Marian, in a pretty violet dress, pink in the cheeks. "Pleased as punch" is how she would have described herself.

Marian. I had been trying not to think about her since my mother first became ill. But it had become more and more difficult not to think about her—as I was doing now. I shut my eyes and opened them. She was still there. Instead of my mother's living room, I saw Marian's living room in Illinois. I saw her standing in the center of the room next to her Victorian sofa, announcing the recurrence of her cancer. She did it in her style—matter-of-fact, chin up, nothing fussy. My mother-in-law was a

small, thin, unsentimental woman with white, perman-
ented hair, clear-rimmed eyeglasses and a schoolteacher's
stance, hands clasped in front and heels together. Her feet
were long and narrow, and she wore English shoes that
buckled or tied. A cardigan sweater sat on her shoulders
without falling off.

Nobody tells lies in my husband's family—the art of
dissembling is unknown to them—and although I never
knew Ed's father, knowing his mother convinced me that
at least half of the tendency toward truthfulness came
from Marian. Her voice was modulated, her manners im-
peccable, but she spoke her mind. "I've never seen the
sense in such-and-so," she'd say to someone who did. The
calm with which she delivered her opinions made you
shiver a little. She could be harsh, yet she was not small-
minded. She was too intelligent to be small-minded, too
self-confident not to be open to another's view.

She didn't trust me at first, when Ed brought me home.
She thought I might be a flashy, New York television
person who would extend a cigarette holder at arm's
length and flick ashes in the palm of her son's hand. When
she realized that (figuratively and literally) I didn't
smoke, she changed her view of me, and a careful but solid
love grew between us. I always felt honored by her love,
because I knew there was nothing automatic about it.

We were at the end of what had been a Norman Rock-
well sort of Thanksgiving. Before I married Ed I hadn't
quite believed holidays or families could be like that. But
there was Ed's family: two undivorced parents with character, three handsome, plucky sons called Bob, Jim, and
Ed, and, when the boys were in short pants, a dog named
Spot.

We had gathered in Marian's living room with our coats
on, about to leave for the airport—Ed's brother Bob was
there, too, along with Bob's wife Gwen and their chil-

dren—when, in a voice so soft we almost didn't hear her, Marian told us. "I hadn't wanted in any way to spoil the lovely time we had together," she said pleasantly, "but I think you should know the doctor has found an inoperable tumor . . ."

After that, her chemotherapy began. It bore no resemblance to the kind my mother got. She received the drugs as an outpatient and afterwards felt weak and tired, but not sick. Once the treatments were over, she had a good spell that lasted a year or so. Then she began to sink. By the time we visited her at Christmas in 1980, she had developed a chronic, debilitating cough and her weight had dropped alarmingly. She still took her daily walk through the park, but watching her from the window of her apartment, we could see what a struggle it was. "Look at her," said Ed, both sadly and proudly. "She's fighting her way across that park. Look at her."

When we visited her a couple of months later, in February, we found her weaker still, coughing more, and in pain. Soon after we arrived, she arranged for us to meet a nurse and a volunteer from Hospice (the home care program for terminally ill people) who, she said, would be helping her, "as things got more difficult." She showed me a list she had made on a yellow legal pad of some of her things—china and silver, mostly—and asked for my help in deciding what to leave to whom. When she saw the look on my face she reassured me that she really did want my help, that she had had a good life and was ready for it to end. I believed her.

The problem was that death did not oblige. The cancer was in her bones. The pain got worse and in the spring she was hospitalized. She had lost so much weight and grown so weak, she could no longer stand. "I didn't want you to see me like this," she told Ed when he went to visit her. And when he left to go off on a professional trip to

Germany, they both expected—and hoped—that they would not see each other again. The doctor said she could "go at any time." It could be a matter of hours, days, he added, probably not as long as weeks. But a month later when Ed returned to New York and called Illinois from the airport, he found out she was merely worse. He went to see her, and this time when he came home he wept.

Morphine kept her out of pain most of the time, but morphine created another problem—severe, chronic constipation. As the rest of her shrunk, her belly swelled like a malnourished child's. She also had to be turned every half hour so as not to develop bedsores. She developed them anyway. Just before Ed left she decided to stop eating, hoping to starve herself to death. She desperately wanted to die, Ed told me, weeping.

But she didn't die.

My mother would ask about Marian, shaking her head at each depressing report. "That poor woman," my mother would say. "That poor woman." Then she'd bemoan her own inability to help. At one point she decided to go to Illinois. With difficulty we finally talked her out of it. My mother and my mother-in-law had met only twice, at our wedding and once again on Marian's last visit to New York. Unpredictably, it was a take. They rendezvoused at our apartment one day before setting out on a lunch date, and I remember thinking that they probably looked as unlike as two people of the same sex and almost the same age can look: my mother, gussied up and even pinker in the cheeks than usual from trying so hard to be liked, and Marian, even plainer in New York than she seemed in Illinois, speaking four subdued words to my mother's four hundred, most of them gushers. But afterwards my mother's gushers included her new friend. "Could a mother of Ed be any different?" On her part, when she got home, Marian wrote a letter to my mother:

"I don't express myself as easily as you do, Ida, but I want you to know I feel all the same things . . ." And they spoke on the phone from time to time, until Marian's sickness made speaking impossible.

When they took Marian home from the hospital, the Hospice home care team went to work, along with other round-the-clock private nurses—all under the management of my sister-in-law, Gwen, who had put her own life on hold. As Marian's pain threatened once again to grow out of control, the dosage of morphine went up. She slept most of the time, but awake she was more than aware of the awful, inert thing her life had become. "I don't understand why I have to go through this," Marian said to her minister when he came to call.

"I don't understand either," he said.

Gwen gave out, finally, and in August she and Bob moved Marian to a nursing home. By then her bones had become so brittle, she cracked a rib from coughing, causing her more pain. She was nothing but pain now, Gwen said. It even hurt when Gwen held her hand. And there was a new problem now. It took more and more morphine to control the pain, but there was hardly any flesh left on Marian's body into which shots could be given. They gave them to her, though, carefully of course, so as not to kill her. Ed went out to see her once again and found her in a morphine haze, coming out of it every so often to pray for death.

Which finally came in September. Too late for grief, not too late for an enduring sadness.

Eleven-thirty now. Soon we'd hear Shany's tap at the door and she'd come in and we'd have our whispered conference in the living room ("She's sleeping. It was better than, worse than, the same as last time. No, she hasn't had any medication since she left the hospital"). Then, Ed and I would gather up the paper and Shany would relieve us until six or so, when I'd come back to relieve her. Not that Shany wanted to be relieved. "Do me a favor," she'd say in the closest thing I knew to my mother's voice, "Don't come back. I can sleep over. You look tired. Go." And if my mother was awake she'd give it to Shany and me. "Do me a favor. You both look tired. I don't need a baby sitter. Go."

To Shany she would also throw in a "You look terrible." That's how my mother spoke to her sister—and worse, I suspected, when I wasn't around. My mother loved Shany and would have done anything for her. They were as fused as a mother and daughter, but fused or not, my mother continually gave Shany the business and Shany took it. So if my mother had all of a sudden got sweet with her, Shany probably would have worried. She was worried enough about my mother without her turning sweet.

A good Sunday after a chemotherapy weekend was one that did not include nighttime throwing up. Most Sundays were not good. And of course Sunday affected Monday. A good Sunday held the possibility of a Monday in which a slice of toast would go down. Otherwise Monday was liquids, and toast got postponed to Tuesday. By Wednesday, depending on Tuesday, Monday, and Sunday, small amounts of "regular food"—cottage cheese, eggs, cooked fruit—might be digested successfully. And by Thursday she could occasionally get through something that passed for a normal meal on her date with Alvin.

"I won't be able to eat much," she'd tell him on the phone Thursday morning.

"What is that, a threat or a promise?" he'd say, and get a little smile out of her.

The Thursday Night Date, if it came off, officially marked the end of the chemotherapy weekend. Shany always called me Friday morning. "Did she go?" She didn't ask my mother herself because my mother would have snapped her head off. Alvin was one of those touchy subjects that was off-limits to Shany, who had remained alone since her husband's death. Nothing in Shany's character would have led her to judge my mother—or me—for our romantic transgressions. But nothing in my mother's character would have wanted to grant her the opportunity. Meanwhile, if on Friday morning I could answer yes, to the date question, we knew we could breathe easy.

Until the next time.

"It'd be better if I didn't know what was coming," my mother said more than once that year. Some understatement that was. Even *I* woke up in a sweat a few days before each treatment. What must those nights have been like for her?

I don't know. I'll never know. She kept that from me. If she could have, she would have kept it all from me.

"Look what I'm doing to my children," she'd say. "The last thing I ever wanted was to do what I'm doing to you."

Naturally, we said all the right things back. "Mother, getting sick isn't your fault. Mother, think of all the times I got sick and you helped me. Mother, don't be silly; Ed's not teaching today, anyway . . ." But she didn't buy it, and I knew why. She felt double-crossed. Her illness had betrayed her and, worse, made her betray us. Mothers are supposed to give care, not get it, not need it. She forgave neither the illness nor herself.

Meanwhile I had no wish to be a martyr. It's a role that might have interested me twenty, thirty years earlier when my mother, something of a martyr herself in those days, had me in a guilt trap. It would have been nice during that stage to flip the trap over, open the door, and put her in my place. But the trap had been inoperative for so many years I couldn't even remember what it felt like, and now the last thing I wanted her to feel along with everything else was guilt about me. I knew, too, that beyond a certain point I couldn't help her. I couldn't fix her cancer. There was no dam I could erect to stop the waves of nausea.

At some point I must have absorbed the fact of my own uselessness because I found myself trying to stay away more, especially from the hospital. I instructed myself to let Shany take over, Pearl, the aide, my cousin Elaine, whomever. But, like a drinker who vows to go on the wagon and—small surprise—doesn't, I couldn't stay away. And again, it wasn't martyrdom but self-interest. Particularly during the very bad times, I felt less agitated being there and seeing her tortured than not being there and imagining it.

How good, I'd think sometimes, that my father missed this. I remembered how he withered when I got sick. I remembered how, in the hospital as my mother fussed with the flowers, he flattened himself against the wall. "Sit down, Leon," my mother ordered. But he didn't want to sit down. He didn't even want to put down his hat and coat. It was as if he had wandered into the wrong room. It broke my heart seeing him that way. My father was a child and children shouldn't be made to see sickness; it can make them grow up before they should. And there was something about my father—his charm, his innocence, his hopefulness—that made him an eternal child. He shouldn't have had to see sickness ever.

My mother and my father met at a party in the neighborhood on a muggy summer evening in 1930. She was twenty-two; he was twenty-seven. My mother heard my father before she saw him. As she walked into the party, escorted by her brother Louis, a Russian song wafted in from the fire escape, onto which most of the party seemed to have spilled. The voice, a beautiful tenor, belonged to someone she couldn't quite see. The instrument he was playing sounded like a guitar but turned out to be something smaller and more peculiar—a balalaika.

The singer raised his head, and in a flash she caught sight of his face. He was dark and handsome—a foreigner, she guessed—with a fiercely charming smile that made his eyes wrinkle. My mother stared, her spine became as rigid as a girder, and Ida the steady one, Ida the smart and practical one, received an arrow straight to the heart.

My father always said that he, in turn, was struck that evening by my mother's big black eyes. Maybe. But it's my guess that he was just as struck by her feet on the ground. You fall in love, an analyst I knew once said, when the unconscious figures out what it needs and goes for it. My father was a Russian immigrant. He got here by sneaking across the Russian border with a forged passport and made his way to Paris, where he hung out until a relative came through with enough money to get him the rest of the way. My father sang songs, picked up instruments and languages, loved a good party and a good joke (and a bad joke), and had virtually no ambition, save to live in a place where neither the Tsar's army nor the Bolsheviks could get him and to have enough money to eat and have a party once in a while. My father was a sprite, but a sprite with sense. He knew that, for a partner, he would be best off with a soul that complemented his. In other words, a rock. In other words, my mother. In my mother, my father's unconscious knew he had a woman who, if she wanted more from life than he provided, would get it herself. And aside from his good looks, my mother sensed in my father someone who wouldn't get in her way when she went after what she wanted, which was indeed More.

They both underestimated a couple of things. She underestimated how irritated she would feel when every time she said "Let's . . . (invest in this, sell that, visit here, study that)," he'd say "What for?" And he underestimated how much he'd wind up running alongside her, even though he didn't want to get anywhere. He surely could not have predicted how his aversion to my mother's efforts to advance would pale next to his aversion to my mother's displeasure.

When they first married, my father was working in his older brother Harold's hardware store. It didn't take long for my mother to size up Harold and figure, correctly, that he wasn't paying my father anything like a decent wage. My mother knew my father couldn't have much money. She expected their financial footing to be shaky at first. She wondered *how* shaky, but she waited until after the wedding to ask to see his bankbook. He laughed. Bankbook? He had no bankbook. But where, she inquired, did he keep his money? Money? He laughed again, pulling the pockets of his pants inside out to punctuate the joke. My mother looked at the worn lining and at the few cents that fell to the floor and tried not to cry and failed. "You mean you have *nothing?*" she said.

"I have you," he said.

My father didn't work for Uncle Harold long. My mother saw to that. She, herself, left Beth Israel and got a better-paying job with a construction company called Joseph Brooks and Co. Joe Brooks was a big, burly Irishman with a terrible temper and a big heart, and he was crazy about my mother. He thought she was a smart Jew and called her Silverman (not Miss or Mrs., just Hey, Silverman). Brooks paid my mother well and she saved the money, and under Brooks's guidance invested it in a small office building in the Bronx. And one day when my father

wasn't looking (in that sense, my father was never looking) she installed him in that building in the last thing he
wanted—his own business. It was a wholesale hardware
business like his brother's, which eventually expanded to
include rubber products and plumbing specialties.

The funny thing was, my father took to it. He even became something of a tyrant, but he had such a good time
being a tyrant—he especially loved to yell at everyone—
that no one who worked for him took his carrying on
seriously. Sometimes they even yelled back. It was a
noisy place.

My mother had a beautiful sign made for the outside. It
read L. Rollin and Company in huge brass letters. My father got a big kick out of that sign. He'd stand outside
sometimes and look at it and grin. Then he'd go inside and
yell some more.

At some point my father stopped asking what all of this
income-building was for because he found out—me. Originally it was supposed to be for all of their children, but it
turned out they couldn't have any more. So I got it all.
This, as the saying goes, proved to be a mixed blessing.

From the start, my mother wanted for me the same
thing her mother had wanted for her, the same thing most
mothers want for their children. At least it had the same
name—the Best. The only difference between my mother
and most others was the lengths she'd go to to get it.
There was the time, for example, she appeared on Alger-
non Black's doorstep in Riverdale. As head of the Ethical
Culture Society, he had a say (so at least my mother
thought) as to whether I would be admitted to the Fieldston Ethical Culture School, which, according to my
mother's research, was the Best school. My mother had already put me through a three-month grilling in prepara-
tion for the entrance examination and now, having

wedged her foot inside the Black house, my mother went to work on both Dr. Black and his wife.

The following fall I began classes at Fieldston.

My mother's Best included, but did not emphasize, goods. As a child I had nice clothes to wear, but nothing fancy—no bunny fur coats or French dresses. I had many dolls, but they were all from the middle class. Their clothes, like mine, were workaday and nothing liquid issued from any of their orifices.

My mother's Best meant education primarily, but education included Culture, and Culture in turn meant lessons. Not only piano lessons, but dancing lessons, acting and elocution lessons, and art lessons. These were not just any old dancing, acting and elocution, and art lessons. Each establishment where I received lessons had the recommendation of the now defunct Child Study Association, my mother's chief source when it came to deciding what direction to shove me in next. In addition, she did virtual security checks on each teacher.

Most of the lessons happened on Saturday in Manhattan. We got there on the subway, a safe place in the 1940s, even for children. My mother would hold my hand on the rumbling platform, and we'd make our way from lesson to lesson, starting with ballet in a brownstone studio on West Sixty-seventh Street and ending with art in a Greenwich Village loft.

Sometimes at the end of the day, instead of going right home, we'd take a subway that stopped near my father's office on East 149th Street. He'd pick us up there and we'd go to an ice cream parlor called Addy Vallin's. (Ice cream, in spite of its high sugar content, was a dietary transgression my mother allowed.) There were booths at Addy Vallin's, but we preferred sitting at the counter. We'd take our places on the shiny red stools—my mother, me in the middle, and my father—and order ice cream sundaes. My mother always chose coffee with chocolate syrup, my father liked chocolate with chocolate, and I had black raspberry. Then we'd taste each other's and make *mmmm* sounds, vowing to have that kind next time, though we usually stuck to our favorites.

I loved those Saturdays. I didn't envy the kids on the block who got to stay home and play and ride their bikes, and I didn't feel pressured by the demands of all the classes. It was fun doing *tours jetés*, even if the muscles in my calves hurt the next day, and I couldn't wait for spring when we took our easels out into Washington Square Park and drew pastels of the trees and the birds, and I adored playing Amy the year we did *Little Women* in dramatics class.

It might have been otherwise, had my mother had a different attitude about the classes, particularly if she had been critical, say, or overserious about my performance in them. But she saw the classes as edifying treats—as cultural forays, good for their own sake. She also complimented me a lot. She hung my terrible pictures, not on the refrigerator door, but in the living room (and, over my protests, kept them in all the living rooms she had until she died). I didn't find out how terrible they were until I grew up, but by then I had enough self-confidence from once having thought they weren't terrible to shrug and move on.

To her credit, my mother did not dole out praise in small, wrapped packages for my eyes only. She sprinkled it around like the good fairy. She sprayed gold dust on all the children. Whenever there was a performance or a recital or a showing, she applauded not only me but the others as well—especially the ones, she'd explain to me later, who needed it most. These were the poor little rich kids whose parents didn't always show up at recital time, so my mother did double duty.

As it turned out, my mother's teaching career never came to much. She did some teaching between Beth Israel and Brooks, and in later years she worked as a substitute, mostly in Harlem. But she didn't stick with it. She was too busy making money, and far too busy with her only child. All the same, throughout her life, other children rarely failed to get her attention—particularly the ones who weren't getting much attention from anyone else.

In the early years of my childhood we lived in a small house in Yonkers, a less than chic suburb of New York. In my mother's eyes, however, Yonkers might have been Oyster Bay. With its big trees and little houses, it was the best sort of place, she knew, to bring up a child. With the help of her mentor, Joe Brooks, she had found a house at a good price in a nice Irish working-class neighborhood. Clark Street held ten neat, small houses on one side, ten on the other. Ours, number forty-four, looked like a child's drawing of a house—a brick square with white shutters and a small front lawn on which my mother had placed one plaster of Paris mother duck and three babies.

It's too bad there weren't any more ducks inside the house. Even with the strays she took in, my mother had more mothering in her than she had objects to mother, so, inevitably, too much of it fell on me. My mother's notions of motherhood were no more casual or relaxed than her notions about food. And as Her Only Child, I was the only dish in her grand, maternal meal plan—the meat, potatoes, brussels sprouts, salad, and fruit-for-dessert all rolled into one.

My bedroom window faced the front of the house. Sometimes at night I'd look out at the O'Sullivan house across the street. The shade in the kids' room would be pulled. But I didn't need to see in. I knew there were three of them in there and two more in the back bedroom, and I knew about the swell time they must've been having. Even more than I envied those kids their siblings, I envied the way their mother—compared to mine at least—didn't pay attention to them.

We all had to be good, of course, but I had to be extra good. Not so much in the sense of being well behaved—in fact I remember little emphasis on anything so well defined or easily accomplished as manners—but good in a bunch of bewildering, sometimes contradictory ways. I had to be smart, for example, but just as important, I had to look nice. My mother drilled me in fractions, and at the same time used a curling iron on my hair. She criticized me indiscriminately and flattered me just as indiscriminately. She encouraged me to think my own thoughts and be independent, but not of her. She enrolled me in assimilated schools, but she expected me to retain fully my— her—Jewish identity. She taught me honesty, but when I returned the kisses and hugs of my aunts and uncles and third cousins, she expected me to look as if I meant them even when I didn't.

There were some advantages of being her daughter. For one, I could have the children on the block over any time I wanted, especially in the summer. My mother would put on her flowered teacher's smock and organize games in the backyard. And when it got very hot, she'd spray us with the garden hose, and everyone squealed and shouted and had a wonderful time. Those kids thought I was the lucky one and in a way I knew I was.

Our relatives, meanwhile, never understood what we were doing in a Catholic enclave. Nor did they ask. They knew my mother did not enjoy cross-examination. But every once in a while someone got brave, usually Sarah's husband, Harry, and uttered a disapproving and audible silence. Which my mother would ignore.

My mother kept advancing in her job with Brooks, whom I called Grandpa. Brooks had a big new contract to build all the automats in New York for Horn & Hardart, and my mother became his chief assistant. Brooks was a reverse bigot. He thought Jews were smarter than anyone else, and he congratulated himself regularly for having hired one. "Silverman!" he'd bark. "Goddamnit! How come you people got all the brains?"

Grandpa Brooks and his small, sweet mouse of a wife and his pack of children lived in Yonkers too, but in a richer, Jewish neighborhood a few miles away. When a house two doors from his went on the market he urged my mother to buy it—advanced her some money too, I think—and she did. The house had more character than our little box on Clark Street—higher ceilings, bay windows, molding—and it became my mother's new obsession. She went about decorating the place as if it were Versailles. All kinds of new words entered her vocabulary—*swatches, conversational groupings, Roman shades*. At the age of twelve, I became her partner in the project, voting on colors with names I had never heard of—*moss* and *mauve*—cheering on her every purchase.

Then one day a letter came from the city announcing the New York Thruway and the necessity of tearing down four houses in its proposed path. These included Grandpa Brooks's and ours. My mother, by nature more pragmatist than protestor, decided not to fight City Hall. Instead, she figured out a way to beat City Hall. She bought Brooks's house from the city for a dollar—it was square and easier to move than ours—and moved it to a new, nicer location nearby. With the money she collected from the city for our house, she came out ahead. Brooks, meanwhile, shook his head, ran through one of his reverse-bigot litanies, and bought a new house a few blocks away.

The entire neighborhood and the local press turned out for the move. As the house rolled slowly through the streets, kids ran after it as if it were a circus elephant. People came out on their doorsteps and cheered. It was a wonderful day for everyone but my father, who thought this time, for sure, my mother had gone too far.

My mother got more than money from her job with Grandpa Brooks. To be the only woman in that big-man, big-cigar business world tickled her pink. And Brooks made her feel smart; she liked that. The job should have at least partially distracted her from me. It didn't. I don't think it was anything personal; that is, nothing about me in particular made her that way. She just seemed to have some kind of maternal motor in her body that kept running the way refrigerators do.

The tone of my mother's mothering changed over the years. Sometimes she was more critical, sometimes less, sometimes not at all. During the last ten years of her life she virtually smothered me with approval. But the intensity of her mothering never changed. The intensity of my mother's mothering was Intense.

She worried less than one would have thought. Perhaps because worry implies frozenness, and to some degree, helplessness. My mother rarely felt helpless. Before she would allow anything as terrible as helplessness to occur, she took action to prevent it. When I was a baby, for example, instead of worrying about germs in public places, she simply didn't take me to public places. She handled the germ-carrying capabilities of friends and relatives in a similar way. During my infancy friends and relatives were permitted to make a fuss over me, but only from a distance.

In part my mother worried less than other mothers because of her innocence. When I began having dates, my mother didn't worry about sex because sex was out of the question. (In the early fifties sex *was* out of the question, but not quite as out of the question as my mother thought.) For her, I was no more likely to go to bed with a boy than I was to hold up a bank with a sawed-off shotgun.

My mother didn't see this as a strategy, but it worked as one. Her assumption had the effect of keeping me out of anyone's bed but my own throughout college (the less than conservative Sarah Lawrence, in Bronxville, New York) long after most of my friends had taken the plunge. Of course most of my friends' mothers weren't living within three blocks of the colleges they attended. My mother had been very understanding about my wish to board at college. She also expected me—and my father—to be understanding about her wish to move to Bronxville. I lived at school, but so in effect did my mother.

Notwithstanding my virginity, college marked the beginning of an inevitable, long rebellion, me against her. I started small, not by sleeping with boys but by having odd friends. When Thanksgiving rolled around, for example, I did not bring home a nice Jewish princess from Baltimore. I brought home Yoko Ono.

Actually, Yoko was a little flower then, and my mother found her charming, but Yoko was only the warm-up. Lorna, who became my best friend, was not charming, not even in my view. The sound of Lorna's voice (something between a screech and a whine) plus the way she smelled (slightly rancid) meant that she had a continual wide berth around her. Except for me. The sight of her was equally unendearing. She had a facial tic and orange hair, and every other fingernail was painted green. She almost never went to class and hid men in her room and played rock 'n' roll all night and finally got expelled. When they came to ready the room for a new girl they found behind Lorna's bookcase a dead mouse, face down, in a pool of strawberry jam.

"Don't think I don't know why you're friendly with Lorna," my mother said.

"Okay, why?"

"To upset us. What other reason could there be?"

"I suppose it never occurred to you that I *like* Lorna."

Pause. Sigh. "It occurs to us all the time."

After Lorna there were others, fifties beatniks or pseudo-beatniks—I didn't really know the difference or care as long as they were dirty and disagreeable. The day I graduated from college I moved to Greenwich Village, got a job acting in an off-Broadway play, and promptly began an affair with an actor. He wasn't as grimy as I would have liked—he went to Yale—but at least he was Christian and drank.

Meanwhile my mother didn't stop loving me. She just suffered, so naturally I hated her. She noticed that I hated her, so she suffered more. And I suffered, too, from guilt. Finally I did what all neurotic New York Jewish girls do who hate/love their mothers. I got psychoanalyzed. By then I had moved into a new stage of rebellion. I no longer presented my unsuitable friends to my mother. I presented no one. I excluded her from my life. She, the steady date of my childhood—I wanted nothing to do with her. I wanted a divorce. She thought she had lost me. She hadn't of course, as I found out on the analyst's couch. My mother ran me just as she had throughout my childhood, but her command post was inside my head now, where I had unwittingly moved her.

The off-Broadway romance with the actor lasted about

five minutes (besides "Christian and drank" he was also gay), so along with two college chums I moved into a gloomy, high-ceilinged apartment on West End Avenue, which we decorated with our mothers' attic furniture. That lasted ten minutes. The ink on the lease had barely dried when I gathered my all-black wardrobe and hoop earrings and moved into a tenement with a thin, blond painter (this one *looked* gay, but he was only hungry) on East Twenty-fourth Street.

My roommates were impressed—this was 1958, before people lived with people—until they realized that I intended to keep my new living arrangement a secret from my parents. Every time my mother called they had to whip up fast lies about where I was, which annoyed them and tormented me because I kept worrying they wouldn't lie right and she'd find out. "And then what?" my analyst would ask, trying in vain to expunge my terror. "Will she beat you? Kill you? What will she do to you?"

In fact, my mother did not call me much. Calling me wouldn't have given her what she wanted. She didn't want to know where I was. Probably she knew and did what she always did about disagreeable facts—turned from them and fixed her eyes instead on the horizon, like a person on shipboard trying to avoid seasickness. No, what my mother wanted from me she couldn't get by calling. My mother wanted me to love her, and she couldn't get that even from my calling her. She couldn't seem to get that, period. And she didn't know why. I didn't either. Neither of us grasped what seems simple now—that no person loves her parole officer.

The solution would have been some sort of reciprocal disengagement. But neither of us knew how to disengage, at least not from each other.

In surgery nowadays, they sometimes use stitches that needn't be severed but which, of their own accord, dissolve. That's what must have happened to my mother and me, because I don't remember a separation taking place. I only remember being aware that it had happened. One day I realized I loved her, and it seemed a nice way to feel. I caught myself calling her on the telephone, because, of all things, I felt like it. Sometimes my calls surprised her. "Oh Betts!" she'd say, trying not to sound too pleased, "I thought you were going to be tied up all day! Nothing went wrong, did it?" "No, I just thought I'd say hello to my favorite mother." I'd hear myself say that and think, who said that? And judging from the stunned silence that followed, my mother was probably asking herself the same question.

Then, in 1975, I remember waking up in a hospital room, having just had a cancerous breast removed. I saw my mother through a drugged haze, and I knew I not only loved her but needed her. And I remember noticing that needing her felt all right too, and I knew the reason it felt all right must be that I had succeeded in separating myself from her.

But I'm not giving enough of the credit to her. She had done a lot of letting go herself, unwillingly at first, then willingly when she saw she was in greater danger of losing me if she didn't let go. I hadn't told her or my father about the surgery in advance. I saw no point in worrying them, since the lump in my breast might have turned out to be benign. So they didn't get a call until the surgery was over and the verdict in. And when the drug fog cleared, the mother I saw standing next to my bed was the mother I remembered from my childhood—the one with the teacher's smock and the bright eyes, the one with the let's-roll-up-our-sleeves-and-lick-this-thing look on her face. No tears, no sorrow, no poor us.

In the part of the brain that houses still photographs, there's one of my mother in that hospital room arranging some yellow tulips on the windowsill. When, in my mind, the shutter clicked, light from the window was shining on her forehead and hair, and I remember thinking how pretty she looked and that I loved her and a calm came over me that felt like a spring breeze, and the years of warring seemed so distant and the warriors like two other people, not us. She turned from the tulips then and moved toward me and kissed me softly on the forehead.

7

chapter

No one expected that final, eighth Sunday we brought her home—on a dark, frigid morning in January—to feel like a celebration. But I think we expected it to be better than it was. "It's over, it's over," I whispered to her on the way home, pressing her limp, cool hand in mine. But the sight of her—the swollen face, the dry mouth, the glassy look in her eyes, the way the flesh on her arms and legs (she had lost thirty pounds) hung from the bone: no matter what it said on the program, this was not to be a day of rejoicing. Happiness, I learned on that occasion, requires a positive event; the conclusion of a negative one doesn't do it. No longer feeling bad is not the same as feeling good.

All the same, feeling good in a gentle sort of way can happen down the road. With a we'll-see prognosis, weeks turned into months, and the cancer monster stayed away. My mother began to get fat again—what a lovely sight it was to see her eat ice cream and look naughty doing it—and life once more began to feel friendly.

Friendly doesn't mean the same as before. It's a special kind of peace that follows war. Special, that is to say, different. Something had permanently changed. Cancer does that. Before cancer you know you're going to die of something someday. But you know this through gauze, the way a drunk at a bar knows where the door is.

After cancer you know where the door is. And no amount of alcohol or turning away keeps you from knowing. Every person who has cancer has a favorite fantasy—to die of something else. Yet even when cancer goes away, even when they use a powerful rat poison (chemotherapy) to make it go away, cancer cells, like rats, tend to return. And multiply. And eventually kill.

Didn't I know that myself? I knew it and lived with it; I know it and live with it still. Living with it means being a little bit scared at least some of the time. It means every time you get, say, a sore throat you think maybe It's in your throat. Then you scold yourself, That's silly, it's only a sore throat. Everyone gets sore throats. And soon your throat stops hurting and it turns out it was only a sore throat. So you relax. Until the next sore throat.

It's a matter of trust—the sudden lack of it. Your body's always been your friend, but now it has betrayed you and you can never feel the same way about it again.

That's how cancer is, even with a good prognosis. Compared to my mother, I had nothing to worry about. I had a good kind of cancer. I never even had chemotherapy. A metastasis from breast cancer can kill you like any other kind, but if they catch the disease early and lop off the breast—or the lump—in time, you might get to live out your life. Or you might not. So what do you do? You try not to think about it. You try not to remember what you know.

"What's remission?" my mother asked me as she picked up her menu at lunch one day.

"Why do you ask?"

"Fay" (a friend, rapidly on her way to becoming an ex-friend) "says I'm in remission. What's she talking about? I hate that word *remission*. It sounds like *intermission*. I think she feels like a big shot using words she doesn't understand. I'll have the chicken salad."

She knew what it meant and she was frightened, not of death, but of cancer death; frightened, not of expulsion from life, but of being grabbed and tortured first.

All the same, my mother was still my mother. As soon as she recovered from the final treatment she moved right back into her I'm-so-lucky mode, as if she had just returned home after doing time in prison to find her roses in bloom. Unsurprisingly, the first sounds she made were the old songs about us. "Please don't say son-in-law. Does a son-in-law give up weekends the way my Ed did? Find me a *son* who does that! And who has a daughter like my Betty? What daughter would . . ." and so on to the chorus and refrain. There was also a new note, a new sentence frame into which she inserted what seemed like an infinite variety of pictures. "I never thought I'd (buy a birthday present, feel so good, have lunch with my daughter, see the inside of a Bloomingdale's dressing room, worry about someone *else*, be myself) again."

By March her energy, her weight, and her hair had all returned. Once more she stood, vertebrae stacked high, like Lucy at her lemonade stand, doling out sympathy and advice to family, friends, and strangers in city buses. She became Shany's bossy older sister again, Elaine's favorite aunt, Rose's best friend, Alvin's best girl. Her vanity regrew with her hair. "Look at this," she said, surveying the lack of gray in the mirror with her old phony annoyance. "They'll still think I dye it."

When my friends asked about my mother I responded automatically in that how-are-you-fine way that people do. "She's well," I'd say, "never better." Then one day I realized it was true. It was really true. Oh my, how thankful I felt, how thankful we all felt. And no one was more thankful than my mother, who had moved into that phase, as a cancer patient, of hearing about this person and that person who had what you had and didn't make it.

"It's not fair," she said more than once, and I think she meant it, "that young people go and an old lady like me keeps hanging around." And with that she returned full circle to her old guilt over how much she liked hanging around, a guilt that in no way spoiled the good time she had doing it.

Disease is rude. Aside from everything else it does, it interrupts. But in 1982, it seemed, the interruption was over. My mother resumed her life and we resumed ours. We traveled; we had late, talky dinners with friends; we went back to work. Neither of us had stopped working during my mother's siege, but I certainly worked less. Fortunately, mine was the kind of professional life that could easily absorb neglect.

In 1982 I had a job doing special (that meant occasional) reports for the late-night ABC news program, "Nightline." The program focused on a different topic each night, usually the big story of the day. But on some days there was no big story and that's where I came in. My beat was Domestic Suffering. No one but me called it that, but the name fit. Whenever they wanted a piece on disease, rape, abuse, and misery, they'd call me and I'd run off—with a producer and camera crew—to shoot a four- or five-minute piece that would lead into the discussion part of the program.

It was a great job. I loved suffering as a beat. To me, no stories were more fascinating or closer to the bone. They almost always involved ordinary people—as opposed to politicians—the sort who, when you interview them, look into your eyes and tell you the truth. Since there is rarely any urgency about getting such stories on the air, one can also take a decent amount of time to do them, even spend time thinking about them, a luxury in television news.

I fell into suffering by accident. For years, working on magazines—*Look* mostly—I wrote the usual stuff about the Beatles and Johnny Carson. Occasionally I did something on divorce and drugs (these *were* the sixties after all), but mainly I stuck to froth. Partly it had to do with a lack of self-confidence; in spite of my mother's early indoctrination, I didn't think I was smart enough to write anything serious. And partly it had to do with where women were in those years. (Nowhere.) So I was never assigned to anything weighty. In the meantime I got good at froth and even whipped up a few frothy books—one on marriage vows, one on funny mothers, and one on not drinking.

In the seventies, I moved into television, became a correspondent for NBC News, and I kissed froth good-bye. Not that NBC sent me to Vietnam, or even to Washington. I had made it clear that I didn't want to go to either of those places. I had no interest in danger or in politics, and since everyone else did, they left me alone. Instead I covered the news in the northeastern United States, and when they allowed me to do more and more feature stories—like rape, hard-to-adopt children, and campus homosexuality—I found out something the boys (and some of the girls) in the newsroom didn't know: that features could be as "serious" as hard news—often more so because they didn't end when the fire went out.

When, a few years later, I got breast cancer and wrote a book about it (*First, You Cry*), that did it. After that, like it or not, I was in suffering for good.

The year before my mother got sick I decided I didn't like it—at least that I had had enough and needed a break. That's when I began working on *Am I Getting Paid for This?*, which turned out to be a more or less cheerful autobiographical book about journalism. I finished the book sometime before the end of my mother's chemotherapy and at the same time began the "Nightline" job, which, mercifully, involved only about a week or two a month. Now, with the chemotherapy over, I felt like working in television again; I felt interested in other people's problems the way I hadn't for a while. So I was pleased to hear on my answering machine one evening that "Nightline" had called with an assignment. Then I found out what the assignment was—Hospice. Hospice was the organization providing services for terminally ill people that my mother-in-law had used (they were wonderful and, needless to say, blameless for what had happened to her). The program's special mandate is to keep dying patients as comfortable as they can be, if possible in their own homes. At the same time, no attempts are made to prolong life through means which usually cause pain and suffering—means like chemotherapy.

I love Hospice; I had done Hospice stories before for NBC. But it was the last story I felt like doing now. Particularly when the producer told me the patient he had lined up for me to interview was a woman dying of cancer.

I did it anyway. I had to. Or I felt I had to. Or something. And it turned out to be not as grim as I expected, not, in fact, grim at all.

The woman's name was Tootsie. She was a seventy-five-year-old retired telephone operator from Chicago, and she had lung cancer which had metastasized to the brain. We went to see her in Atlanta where she lived with her nephew and his wife. They, along with the Hospice people, were taking care of her. I had already deduced that the nephew and niece had to be saintly, but when they told me that Tootsie was no burden, that in fact they liked having her around, I thought they might be crazy as well.

One look at Tootsie and I knew I was wrong. We found her in her bedroom, frail and toothless but sitting erect in a chair, decked out in a purple angora sweater and pants, finishing off a beer and a cigarette. Her brain worked only in spurts; her answers were short, but she made herself clear nevertheless. When I asked her how she had reacted to a doctor who wanted to give her more chemotherapy beyond the point where it made any kind of sense, she looked me in the eye and told me what she told him, "The hell with that!"

Tootsie, in short, was a sketch. She died without pain a month later.

Ed had a Guggenheim Fellowship that year. *The New York Times* announced it, but they needn't have. My mother had already told the world. The fellowship gave Ed a break from teaching and a subsidized year to work on a book he was doing about a nineteenth-century algebraist named Galois. Here, too, was an opportunity to exercise some of his mathematical wanderlust, and after Tootsie we both decided to exercise a little geographical wanderlust as well. In March we took off for a part-work trip to the Southwest, where the colors alone made us giddy.

Ed gave talks at the Universities of Arizona and New

Mexico. I attended, comprehending nothing, but enjoying the sight of my husband waving his arms about, intoning his beloved formulas, attacking the blackboard with the chalk, leaving there assemblages of numbers and symbols which the hairy, sockless Southwestern topologists seemed to find enthralling.

We moved on to Denver, where it was my turn. I addressed a women's group about working in the "soft" side of journalism. From there, home, just in time to muscle in on my mother's Thursday night date with Alvin. We met them at Shun Lee on Fifty-fifth Street. I couldn't believe it. Alvin actually had my mother eating Chinese food.

"Some of the vegetable dishes are very nutritious," she said in her old healthier-than-thou tone.

Ed and I worked most of that summer, taking off weekends to visit friends in the country. At the end of August we drove up to Cape Cod and holed up for a week in Chatham, a lovely, misty town where we knew no one and passed the time lolling on the beach and reading under trees and playing Scrabble and writing and doing mathematics. (Anyway, half of us did mathematics.)

Notwithstanding all of life's ongoing global and national horrors, our own life, within its narrow confines, seemed extraordinarily good that summer. Work was going well. Ed wound up his fellowship year by finishing his book on Galois. My book, *Am I Getting Paid for This?*, would be published soon, and I had a new extremely unboring television assignment—a profile of a pathological killer.

And the other part of life wasn't bad, either. Our marriage, now nearing its fifth year, had turned out to be the kind I never expected to have because I am hard-headed and know not to expect the moon. Yet there was the moon out there in the kitchen every morning squeezing fresh orange juice. How, as my mother said, did I get so lucky? And speaking of my mother, she had been well, really well, for more than eight months. And so was I well, a fact which I had stopped taking for granted in 1975 when I had had my own cancer blitz.

In September we had a couple of lovely celebrations—my mother's seventy-fifth birthday, which we managed to get through without any beans spilled about her age to Alvin, and the publication of my book, for which our friends, the Limans, gave a big, wonderful party in their big, wonderful Fifth Avenue apartment. My mother made her entrance on Alvin's arm wearing the same salmon-colored silk dress with ruffles around the neck that she had worn to our wedding. There was such a crowd I didn't see much of her during the party, but Ed told me later how she had worked the room, accepting every hors d'oeuvre offered her, introducing herself to everyone who asked (and everyone who didn't) as the book's grandmother.

No doubt if I thought hard enough I'd remember something bad that happened that year, but nothing comes to my mind. Nor did what happened in June of '83 seem so bad at first. My mother had a stomachache. Well so what, everyone gets stomachaches. Her internist, Dr. Foster, recommended Pepto-Bismol.

A week later the pain hadn't gone away. "It isn't any *worse*," my mother said.

"That's good," I said. And neither of us said what we were thinking.

Another week went by. No change. Then I said it, sort of. "Why don't you ... maybe you should just check in with Dr. Burns. It's probably indigestion, but wouldn't it be nice to hear that from him?"

My mother agreed it would be nice to hear that from

him, and she made an appointment for three weeks, she told me, from that day.

"Three weeks!" I said. "Why three weeks?"

"That's his first opening."

"Did you tell the nurse you were in pain?"

"Yes."

"Did she tell Dr. Burns?"

"She said she did."

"When did you talk to Dr. Foster last?"

"A few days ago."

"What did he suggest?"

"More Pepto-Bismol."

My mother didn't sound like my mother. All those short answers. I thought, She's either sicker than she says or hiding something or just scared. Of course she's scared; she's no fool. She's thinking, This is it, maybe this is it.

I am thinking the same thing.

8

chapter

July 5, 1983. I sit, knees together, on a straight-backed chair in Dr. Burns's waiting room. My mother is inside being examined. The waiting room is jammed. Across from me two women sit on a loveseat, their heads turned in opposite directions, as if that might help create more space between them. One is pregnant. She has a striped bow in her hair and flips through pages of a magazine with a cake on its cover. The other, a woman whose age is difficult to tell, somewhere between fifty and sixty, stares at the air. Her lips are tight, she wears not a trace of makeup, and a cotton scarf is tied tight around her head. I know what that means.

I've been trying to read. I've also been trying not to

look in the direction of the examining room. Suddenly the nurse calls my name. "Dr. Burns would like to see you," she says. I spring up and follow her down the hallway. My mother, dressed, is just coming out of Dr. Burns's office. As she passes me, she says something about stopping at the appointment desk in the foyer. I look for a clue on her face and see none. The nurse leads me into Dr. Burns's office. He is half standing, half sitting on the edge of his desk, his arms folded, his eyes on the floor.

"Well, she has a recurrence," he says, still looking down. "It's in the same area." My head fills with air and I miss the next few words, but I snap to when I hear the word *chemotherapy.*

"We'll put her on a course of three treatments. Then we'll take a look. Then we'll probably want to give her a few more."

"Oh no," I whisper. "Oh no. Not again."

He says nothing. But he stands away from his desk, as if our conversation has ended and all that remains is for me to signal that I understand it has ended so that he can leave the room.

Meanwhile I know too much and what I know is blazing like neon inside my head. I know that at her age, with a recurrence of ovarian cancer, she can't have much time left. I know that chemotherapy might prolong her life a little and that it might not. I know what chemotherapy would do to what's left of her life. And I know about people who say "The hell with that." I remember Tootsie.

I have been struggling to organize myself so that the words I want to say will come out. Finally they do. "Is there any point in putting her through those treatments, Dr. Burns? Are you sure it will . . . help? Are you sure? You know what chemotherapy was like for her. Is it worth it to put her through that again? I mean . . . with a recurrence . . . is there any real hope? Do you *know* it will buy her more time?"

He begins to speak, but I interrupt him. "I know it's her decision, not yours or mine, but she'll listen to you. Can't you . . . does it make sense to put her through that again?"

"We can't do nothing," he says, edging near the door.

"Why not?" I ask. I ask softly, nicely. I know I am irritating him and I don't want to do that. I do not wish to incur the animosity of this man who is the guardian of my mother's life. But I must know the answer.

Or must I? I notice that my questioning leaves off there. I do not get specific. I do not ask the baseline question: How long is she likely to live if she doesn't get chemotherapy? Nor do I ask how long she might live if she gets it. But again I think of Tootsie, and I think of Tootsie's beer, and I do manage to get out a mumbled query about the quality of life, that buzz phrase that no longer seems like a buzz phrase.

Dr. Burns has resumed his survey of the floor. "They're usually a little more comfortable after the chemo," he says.

I wince at the *they*, but he has caught my attention with the word *comfortable*. Yes, he has reached me with *comfortable* and he knows it. I look at him closely and try to see on his face whether this is mere cajolery. But his face, lean and long, is an arrangement of regular features with no discernible affect.

"How can it make her more comfortable to have chemotherapy?"

"Chemotherapy works to shrink the tumor. Your mother's pain is from the tumor."

"But it won't *necessarily* shrink the tumor." He correctly reads this as half question and half statement and elects not to respond.

"What about surgery?" I am reaching now.

He shakes his head. "Surgery is not possible. The tumor is in the abdominal region. It is . . . not confined to a place where it can be removed."

My eyes join his on the floor. My head drops too. I've lost and we both know it. "You say three treatments."

He places his hand on the doorknob. "Well, at least three . . ." He turns it. "Probably six. We take a scan after three. Then we decide. They usually need six."

They. The door is open now.

"One more question, Dr. Burns. Does she know? Does she . . . want this?"

"She seems to," he says. And now he is out of the room.

"Thank you," I say because my mother taught me to say thank you, and I follow him out.

My mother is at the appointment desk, sitting up straight in a chair, her purse in her lap, speaking in soft, agreeable tones to the appointment secretary who has just booked her into the hospital for her first chemotherapy. My mother gets up and I help her on with her coat. So far, we have avoided looking in each other's eyes. In the elevator I work hard to keep down the lump that is lodged in my throat.

I hail a taxi and we get in. She looks out the window and sighs. "Well, it's been a nice year."

This is too much for me, and I break. She does not.

"It's not what I expected," she says a few moments later. "I expected a death sentence. I didn't expect torture. That's a surprise." Her mother's word. She laughs a little.

I go upstairs with her to her apartment. She lies on her bed and I sit on a chair across the room. She shakes her head. "I didn't think I'd have to go through that again. That I didn't expect."

"Mother, you *don't* have to. No one can force you to have chemotherapy. You can decide not to." These words have fallen out of my mouth; too late now to take them back.

She looks at me strangely, almost coldly. "How can I decide not to? It's the only chance I have."

Chance for what? I think. Burns doesn't know. What if it's only a few months? What kind of few months will it be? I know something about this now. An inoperable recurrence in the abdominal region doesn't just go away. But I say nothing. She'd rather be tortured than lose hope. So be it.

She has gotten up and walked to her closet. She is reaching for something on a shelf above her clothes—a box. She opens it and carefully takes out her wig. She looks pleased.

"I'm glad I saved it," she says, and lowers it gently, as if it's a lame bird, back into the box.

9

chapter

I reported all of this to Ed later that evening at home. "She didn't even hesitate about the chemotherapy. I can't understand how she can face that again."

"She must think it's her only chance."

"That's exactly what she said. But she's seventy-five years old. She's got a recurrence of cancer—inoperable cancer. What kind of chance can she have with or without treatment?"

"Did you ask Dr. Burns that?"

"Not really."

"Why not?"

"I don't know. I guess I didn't want to hear the answer. And it's not for me to ask. It's really her question to ask when she's ready, and she's clearly not ready or she'd ask herself. Not, by the way, that Burns necessarily knows the answer. He may have a general idea, but I have a general idea and so do you and so must she. My mother is going to die and she's probably going to die fairly soon and—" I suddenly realized my voice had become shrill and I lowered it. "He did say the chemo might make her more comfortable—shrink the tumor—but that's a maybe. I *know* that's a maybe." We were seated on opposite sides of the living room. The room had grown dark and the lights were off. I got up and walked to the window. "She's not stupid. She knows she can't have any real time left. You'd think she'd want it to be *good* time."

Ed shook his head. "But you're assuming she's ready to call it quits, and she isn't. Not yet she isn't."

I walked back and sat down on the sofa. "You're right," I said, staring at the rug. "She wants those treatments because they might prolong her life a little bit. And she doesn't even want to know how little it might be." I shook my head slowly and looked up at Ed. "I understand but I don't understand. After what she's been through, to face that chemotherapy again? I wouldn't, would you?"

"I don't think I would," said Ed, turning his face toward the window. "But I can't be sure. I don't think you know what you'll do in a situation like that until you're in it yourself."

The routine had changed somewhat. It used to be that she checked into the hospital Friday, got blasted Saturday, and came home Sunday. Now they planned to start the chemotherapy right away early Friday evening and she'd go home Saturday. Shorter is better, I thought, but I didn't want to think what Friday night would be like, or what kind of traveling condition she'd be in when Saturday morning came.

The drug regimen had changed as well. No Adriamycin this time, only cisplatin. Would she therefore get less sick? No one seemed to know. Having left Dr. Foster (after his third recommendation of Pepto-Bismol), she now had a new internist, a young, nice, rather melancholy man with a good reputation, Dr. Goldman. He said he didn't know if she'd have an easier time of it without Adriamycin, and when I asked Dr. Burns he got that glazed that's-not-my-department look he always got whenever I asked him anything that had to do with throwing up. Putting it all together, I figured she'd get as sick as before.

Friday, July 22. The day is perversely beautiful. My mother is in pain. She describes it as a great weight inside her stomach pulling her down. She walks with difficulty, but she is "sure that after the treatment I'll feel better."

Slowly, with her in front of me (has she shrunk? she seems smaller than before) I push the revolving door into the hospital. The admitting office has been moved to the back of the main floor. Otherwise it's the same scene as before, even—can it be?

"You bin here bevore?" It's the little German volunteer with the indefatigable squint. Something in me sinks at the sight of her.

Once my mother is settled in her room, I go up to the private duty nurse office and sign for a nurse's aide for the overnight shift. I ask for Pearl but am told Pearl only works days now and is unavailable. They have someone else though who they're sure will be fine.

Back on my mother's floor, I recognize some of the nurses. In a crazy way it's nice to see them. Pointlessly, I wonder if recidivist criminals feel the same way when they get caught and locked up again. The cheerleader has a new short haircut that makes her look older. Irish is the same. "How are you, dear-r?" she says to my mother.

My mother smiles. "I had a nice year."

There has been a gradual acceleration of noise and activity in my mother's room. The hospital orchestra is tuning up: blood pressure, temperature; extra pillow, extra blanket; ice water; clothes quiz ("How many nightgowns?" "Two." "How many stockings?" "Two."); intern's quiz ("When did you first feel the pain?"). Crank up the bed, crank it down, order TV. The roommate, whose age I can't tell, has a ruddy, round face and a slack mouth and sleeps through it all, snoring.

Dr. Burns makes his appearance surrounded by his white-coated entourage. They stand in a line like the lineup of ducks on our lawn on Clark Street. As they make their quacking noises, what's left of the sunlight shoots through the venetian blinds. At six o'clock the IV pole rolls in and the terrible symphony begins.

But not yet. The intern, who has small craters under his eyes, can't find a vein. He pierces her skin as if he is a carpenter and she is wood. Each time he sticks her with the needle she winces, shuts her eyes tight, turns her head away. My hands are cold but I can feel myself getting wet under the arms. The intern is sweating too. I can see the drops on the side of his forehead as he bends over her hand.

"Oh, please!" The sound of my mother's cry yanks me out of my chair. "Look," I say to him, careful not to shout, careful, too, not to come any closer, careful not to narrow the respectful distance that must be kept between the patient's relative and the physician, careful, above all, not to insult. "You're not the only one who's had a hard time finding her veins. But I really can't let you continue this way. There are a few people around here who seem to have a ... a knack. Would you ... please call someone else?"

He does not look at me as I speak. "I've almost got it now," he mumbles, his back bent like a factory worker over this stubborn appendage, my mother's small white hand, which has now turned blue. He gets up suddenly, excuses himself as he moves past me, walks around to the other side of the bed, and picks up her other hand. My mother looks up at him and begs him with her eyes not to hurt her any more. I'll give him two tries, I say to myself. Two. He gets it on the third. My mother moans with relief. "Thank you," she says to him as he hurriedly packs up his equipment. I say nothing; nor does he. In thirty seconds he is gone.

I notice—and feel guilty that I've noticed—that the Friday/Saturday routine is easier on, if no one else, me. Even if I want to be there during the really bad time, even if I feel morbidly compulsive about it, I cannot be there. Visitors must leave at eight. With the IV going in at six, the vomiting won't begin until midnight.

Only later, much later, at two in the morning and again at three and at four-thirty, do I discover what I forgot from last time, that removing your body from a place is effective only if you remove your mind, and you can't remove your mind unless you're an emotional acrobat. But I try. I try every sleeping trick I know—the one in which you relax each muscle, one at a time; the one in which you say a word over and over. As a last resort, very slowly, I recite the alphabet backwards.

"What's the matter?" says my husband. It is three A.M.

"I'm worried about the aide."

"What aide?"

"The overnight one."

"What are you worried about?"

"I don't know, that she's not doing it right."

"You know what?"

"What?"

"I bet she *is* doing it right. That's much more likely. Think how much more likely that is."

"Okay."

"Now go to sleep."

And for what feels like five minutes before it's time to get up and go to the hospital to pick her up, I do.

10
chapter

The hospital replay continued. In the morning we found her propped up in a chair, eyes half-shut, face swollen and puffy from Thorazine, barely able to hold the plastic dish in her lap.

She was also dressed, made-up, and ready to go.

"Did the aide help you dress?"

She nodded.

"How was she?"

My mother shrugged. "Religious."

We had had one of those the year before. As you throw up they try to convert you. My mother finally told her to knock it off. I asked her if she did the same last night.

She shook her head and mumbled, "Too sick."

By the time Shany came to her apartment at noon, my mother was curled up on her side in one of those mercifully heavy, drugged sleeps she always had after coming home from the hospital. Shany stayed the night and reported to me the next morning that my mother had not only swallowed—and kept down—half a cup of tea, but had eaten three tablespoons of cereal to boot. This was news. In the previous go-round she wouldn't hit solid food for at least two days. "That's great!" I said, and called Ed at his office to tell him.

But by Wednesday the cheering had stopped. On Thursday she canceled her date with Alvin. There was, it turned out, another difference between this time and last—pain, the same pain she had going to the hospital. But worse. She described it as a "weight," a feeling of something very heavy in her pelvic region that pressed hard "like an iron" against everything around it. As a result, she couldn't straighten up or walk. She just lay in bed with her knees up, softly moaning.

"I don't understand," she said. "Dr. Burns said the treatment would help."

"Mother, I'm sure he didn't say *one* treatment would help." And, I thought, I'll bet the next one won't either.

When I got home I called her internist, Dr. Goldman, and asked him what he thought about the chemotherapy. I found Dr. Goldman easy to talk to, the way, it seems, some doctors just are and others, like Dr. Burns, just aren't. I knew Dr. Goldman revered Dr. Burns, so it didn't surprise me when he said that if Dr. Burns advised chemotherapy it probably made sense, and no, he didn't think Dr. Burns was going through motions, and yes, it was certainly possible—if not likely—that the treatments would indeed shrink the tumor and lessen her pain. No way to know that for sure of course. And one more no to my question about whether anything had been invented since her last round of chemotherapy to treat nausea.

As I talked to Goldman I got an idea. It was such an obvious idea that I felt stupid for not thinking of it before. We needed a second opinion, that's what we needed, and we needed it from a cancer specialist, an oncologist.

A few inquiries led, unsurprisingly, to Memorial Sloan-Kettering and to an oncologist there who specialized in ovarian cancer. Great, except we couldn't get an appointment for a month, after her next scheduled chemotherapy. And that wasn't the only problem. My mother didn't want to go. She didn't want to offend Dr. Burns.

"Mother, it's too important to worry about Dr. Burns's feelings!" Wrong tack. I did better with "Dr. Burns doesn't have to know."

But she didn't quite trust me. "Doesn't the new doctor need to see the records?"

"Yes. So?"

"Dr. Burns will find out then."

"Not necessarily," and back and forth we went. Shany and I together finally wore her down with a strong backup from Ed and my cousin Elaine. Meanwhile I had also gone to work on the oncologist's secretary and succeeded in getting my mother an earlier appointment.

Her insides still hurt, but she had figured out two ways of making the hurt less: not eating and not walking. Each time she ate or walked she "paid," as she put it. This had two opposing effects. She seemed buoyed psychologically to have identified what made her feel worse and to have found something she could do, herself, that would make her feel better. This meant that she still had some control. But the "control" all added up to little more than a cruel joke, since eating and walking are no small things to give up—one being essential to life, the other feeling essential to *her* life. So for the first time in memory my mother dropped into a palpable depression. I could hear it in her voice, which became low and oddly hoarse. She would try to smile, but even when she succeeded, it was a wan, ghostly smile.

She looked sicker than she ever had between treatments in the past. Her arms and legs were still fleshy, but the rest of her body had narrowed. Her dresses—on the rare occasions that she felt well enough to put one on—had to be gathered up with belts. And when she walked, the pain made her bend over. Her cheeks became hollow. Her once beautiful dark eyes looked too big now, too staring. I observed these changes, some of which I pretended not to notice, with a sense of helplessness that made me feel as if I were choking. As time passed, medication lessened her consciousness of her pain, but that was not the same, we both knew, as making it go away. The terrible probability had dawned on us both that nothing would make it go away. Pain had moved in for good. Pain now resided in my mother's body, and except for occasional temporary departures, it was never going to move out.

She grew more resigned to the idea of seeing Dr. Fine, the oncologist at Memorial. At one point she even sounded vaguely hopeful about it, going so far as to express the wish that he would recommend surgery. All the same, she wanted to remain Dr. Burns's good girl. She still worried that he might found out about her "date" with the other doctor.

August 6. She forced herself into a kind of command performance for Ed's birthday, fortifying herself with Demerol and codeine and Mylanta and I don't know what else. She ate nothing all day, kept off her feet, and when evening came she covered her face with Charles of the Ritz, and at eight P.M. sharp walked upright on Alvin's arm into the Russian Tea Room.

The evening had a sweet sadness about it. We all tried,

too hard probably, to carry on the way we always had—
like a British acting troupe doing Shakespeare in 1940,
pretending not to hear the bombs. Alvin told his jokes,
which my mother smiled at and didn't get. My mother
clucked over the borscht (even though she ate less than
half of it and nothing else). "Isn't it a pretty color? And
it's very healthy, you know. I wish you kids ate more
soup." I had a glass of wine and talked too much. Ed, as
usual, was the group's star listener.

As the dinner progressed my mother got quieter. Her
pain had obviously returned. It was as if a member of the
Gestapo had suddenly sat down and joined our table. No
one said a word about it, but we skipped dessert and
Alvin got her into a taxi, pretending it was he who had to
go home. "I have an early appointment tomorrow," he
said gallantly. We did our good-bye kisses, and Ed and I
slowly and silently walked across Fifty-seventh Street.

"Alvin's a peach, isn't he?" I said finally.

"Yes," said Ed, in a cracked voice, "Alvin is a peach."

August 11. Dr. Fine startled us. He was a man with all
his windows open. He exuded fresh air, pep, and cheer.
His movements were staccato. He flashed teeth. In spite
of his girth, he hopped about the room like a robin. "Do I
have the X rays or do you? I have them? I don't see them.
Are you sure? Maybe my secretary has them. Delores?
Do we have Mrs. Rollin's X rays? Yes? Oh good . . ."

My balance was thrown, but at the same time I felt relieved. Fine was a Big Gun. From a Big Gun at Memorial
I expected formidability, not fluttering. Fine was almost
cute.

My mother had a different view. The more he hopped,
the more she sank. He located the X rays finally and,
humming a little, began to study them on a lighted screen
on his desk. He had placed my mother on a small, white

stool in the center of the room, where she sat very still in her navy straw bowler (her hair had only just begun to fall out), her pocketbook in her lap. Her shoulders were rounded and her head was down and she looked very small. I knew she hadn't eaten that day, nor anything much the day before, and she had been feeling queasy all morning.

"Are you all right?" I whispered.

She nodded but didn't speak. I know why, I said to myself as my own head began to throb. She thinks it's impolite to say she feels sick.

There was no sound in the room, except for the hum of fluorescents and the scraping of X rays being moved into place on the light box. At last Dr. Fine clicked the light off and turned toward us. "All right, Mrs. Rollin," he said with the geniality of a maître d', "if you'll step this way," and he led her into an examining room.

When they returned, he sat her down on the same stool and sat himself on a chair facing her. He leaned toward her, his elbows resting on his knees, and asked her some questions about her past treatment. Then he leaned back and said what must have been the last thing either of us expected to hear. "My dear lady, I hate to tell you, but what you have had in the way of chemotherapy is a drop in the proverbial bucket. We would have treated you *much* more aggressively here from the beginning, and my recommendation would be to treat you aggressively now."

Jesus.

". . . we don't know, other organs may be involved, so that's why it makes sense to use a number of different drugs, not only the cisplatin. I would suggest that you come for treatments—you can do it on an outpatient basis—once a week or once every two weeks. Each dosage actually would be smaller than the ones you received in the past, but much more frequent."

My mother's mouth had opened slightly. She looked faint.

"You see," he said turning to me with a quick smile, "what we do here is treat patients very aggressively. We bring them close to death and then," he made a scooping motion with his right hand, "we rescue them." Another smile. He turned back to my mother. "Do you have any questions?"

My mother looked at me as if to say, "Speak for me," so I did. "Should we . . ." I began falteringly, not wanting to reach the end of the question; knowing that the answer, whatever it was, would not be good; knowing there were no good answers anymore, only different kinds of bad ones. "Should we assume that surgery is no longer an option?"

"That's right," said Dr. Fine briskly. Once again, he turned toward my mother. His voice was softer now, like a teacher trying to be kind to a slow student. "Do you have any questions, Mrs. Rollin? What are your thoughts?"

My mother looked at Dr. Fine, then at me, then back at Dr. Fine.

"I don't like to tell you in front of my daughter."

"She's a big girl," said the doctor.

"It's all right, Mother," I said.

My mother looked straight at the doctor and in a steady, low voice she said, "What I wish more than anything in the world is that I could take some kind of pill . . . and end this."

Dr. Fine nodded. He'd heard that before. So had I in not so many words. I knew my mother had to be feeling that way. Who wouldn't feel that way? It didn't surprise me. Nor did it alarm me. Because of course she didn't really mean it. But I sobbed inside to think how miserable she must have been to say such a thing.

Dr. Fine rose to his feet. "Well, I know how difficult this has been for you." Standing, he made my mother look even smaller than before.

"Well, thank you," I said, and stood. "I guess . . . we'll have to do some thinking about this."

"If you'd like to begin treatment here," he said, "call my secretary and she'll set up the first appointment."

I helped my mother up and she thanked the doctor and started out the door. I lingered for a moment, trying to decide whether to ask the obvious question. It was clear my mother didn't want to ask it, which meant she didn't want to know the answer. With no time to think and with my mother just now out of earshot, I made the leap. "If she continues the treatments she's been getting with Dr. Burns, what do you think are her . . . chances?"

He won't answer, I thought. They never answer questions like that.

"She has a thirty percent chance of remission, I'd say—no telling for how long—but that's if she continues with cisplatin alone. If the Adriamycin is added," he shrugged, "maybe sixty percent."

I swallowed. The next one, I thought, he will surely not answer. "Do you think Dr. Burns is competent to be giving her these treatments?"

Not even a pause. "Dr. Burns is a very nice man, a very good surgeon." Smile. "But he's a surgeon. He doesn't know about chemistry. We're always telling these fellows, 'Look, you cut. You know about cutting. We're chemists. We know about drugs. Why don't you do your work and we'll do ours?' But they don't listen." Smile.

Burns, you arrogant bastard, I thought. Why did I let her stay with you so long? Why? Why didn't I—

My inner tirade against Burns switched off at the sight of my mother sitting in the new, stooped way she sat now on a bench near the outside door. She faced the window, so I saw only her back. But oh, the sadness in the curve of that back. Oh, how licked she looked. How shrunken and how licked. "She's a very sweet lady, your mother," said Dr. Fine. "I'd be happy to treat her."

"Thank you," I said, "and thanks for being so ... frank."

I walked quickly to my mother, helped her up, and pushed open the big glass door. We were struck by a sudden bolt of sunlight and hot air, as if we had just emerged from an afternoon movie. My mother hardly spoke in the taxi going home. She waited until we had reached her apartment building and were in the elevator. "He had a very good time with us," she said, her lips tight.

"What do you mean?"

"I think he was cruel."

Uh oh, I thought. "I know what you're saying, Mother," I began carefully. "He was awfully *bouncy*. But I think he meant well—"

"*Please,*" she said, interrupting me. She looked angry. I sighed. I knew what *please* meant. It meant the same thing it had always meant—Case Closed. No Dr. Fine, no Memorial. I stared at the elevator inspection sign and wondered, what now? Once in the apartment she headed straight for the bedroom. "I want to lie down. That room was so stuffy I thought I'd pass out."

"Why didn't you say anything?"

"What's the point?" she said, sitting on the bed now and slowly pulling off her shoes. "Do you think he cared how I felt? Can you imagine Dr. Burns acting that way?"

I didn't answer. I just looked at her. Then I helped her out of her clothes and into bed and went home.

11
chapter

"She hated him," I said to Ed. "She absolutely hated him. She didn't even want to consider switching doctors. I didn't dare *mention* it."

We were home, eating a dinner I had cooked with less than consummate skill. I put down my fork. Somehow I had managed to undercook the vegetable and overcook the meat. "The trouble is if I put the beans back, everything else'll get cold."

"Don't worry about it. The beans are fine. Why did she hate him?"

"I don't know. Maybe because he talked to her straight. If only he hadn't been so goddamned cheery about it. These cancer doctors are weird, you know. I guess they have to be. I guess I'd get weird too if I did that for a living. Can you imagine? Having to . . . do you want more butter on your beans?"

"The beans are fine. Did she hear what he said about the Adriamycin?"

"I don't think so. I'm sure she didn't. Anyway, she didn't want to hear, so even if she did, she didn't. I thought about telling her myself. 'Mother, here's the choice. The doctor says if he treats you, you have a sixty percent shot at living, but for how long he can't say. If, on the other hand, you stay with Dr. Burns and he continues to treat you with cisplatin alone, your chances are thirty percent. You decide.' You know something? I couldn't say that to her. According to the book I should have. You know, total honesty and all that. But my sense of her is that she doesn't *want* total honesty. She doesn't want that at all. She doesn't want to be lied to, but she doesn't want the full, raw truth, either. And by the way do you think I was any different? I was no different at all. When I first got cancer I didn't want to know where I stood. I could only handle a little truth at a time. I dealt with losing that breast, and I didn't want to know about dying or *not* dying until much later. Anyway, what do you know when you know? Statistics are just odds. Thirty percent this could happen, sixty percent that could happen. To make decisions based on those numbers isn't science; it's horse racing!"

I put a forkful of beans in my mouth and shut myself up. In the silence, noises from the street rose and seeped through the windows like steam—a too-loud radio, a car horn, another car horn, someone shouting something foul in the garage across the street, the sounds New Yorkers train themselves not to hear. This dinner, I thought, is lousy.

"Near the end of the appointment he asked her if she

had any questions or anything to say, and she said that she wished she could take a tablet and end it all." I put down my fork. "It was awful to hear her say that. Awful."

"So she'll stay with Burns?"

"I guess so. She's attached to him somehow. It's amazing. He doesn't talk to her. He gives her the wrong drugs. And still she won't let go. She's like those abused children who cling to their parents even though they beat them. Burns is her daddy. And whatever I feel about him, I guess I should keep it to myself."

"I think that's right," said Ed, cleaning his plate like a camper. "If she feels so strongly about Dr. Burns, you don't want to do anything to disturb that. Also I think 'the wrong drugs,' is a little harsh. Maybe he has a reason for not using the Adriamycin that you don't know about. And another thing. Fine is talking about blasting her every week or two. I can't see your mother taking that."

"I can't either. Of course if he gave it to her that often he wouldn't give her as strong a dose, but psychologically it would be terrible. Her whole life would be chemotherapy. And for what?"

"That's the question," said Ed, taking his plate into the kitchen. "That's the question."

"You're a good husband," I said.

"Yeah? How come?"

"You'll eat anything."

The next morning I called Dr. Goldman to report to him on the Memorial visit.

"So maybe Fine is wrong about the Adriamycin," I said, "or even if he's right, maybe fighting this thing so hard isn't appropriate anymore. I really think she's worn out and just wants relief from pain at this point. But if she *is* going to get these awful treatments—and I guess she is—maybe she ought to get the Adriamycin. Would you ask Dr. Burns about it? I think it would be better coming from you." Besides, I should have said, I'm too much of a coward to call Burns.

"Sure," he said and we hung up. I let my head fall onto the back of the chair and I looked up at the ceiling and thought, not for the first time, how lucky my father was—how lucky anyone was—to fall down dead of a heart attack.

August 20. Chemotherapy. Bad. Sick going in, sicker going out. No Adriamycin; Dr. Goldman came by Friday evening and said the decision had something to do with the drug being a danger to her heart. So what? I felt like saying. Hard, though, to concentrate on any part of the conversation. Too leveled by the spectacle of this horrible replay—the retching, the bile, the head at a crazy angle on the pillow as if disconnected, the moans. And it was worse than a replay because the horror began early, even before the chemotherapy took full effect.

Then Saturday. The nausea still, the swollen mouth, the drugged eyes, the limp, beaten, bent look of her in a wheelchair, so weak she could barely hold the plastic dish.

It wasn't a good Sunday. Or a good Monday. Or Tuesday. Thursday, better. She kept down a little cereal and a couple of crackers. Date with Alvin out of the question. Too weak. Too much pain. Still the dragging pressure, the pushing pain.

She looked up at me with her big eyes, undrugged now and unblinking. "I thought the chemotherapy would make the pain go away." Mommy, I hurt. Can't the doctor fix it? How, I thought, do parents stand this? How can I? I can't. I can't stand it.

"I don't want it to be the way it was with Marian," she

said in a half whisper, curled on her side like a sick dog. "I saw what that did to Ed. I don't want to do that to my children."

I knew she had to be thinking of Marian. Ed and I had been thinking about her too. She was right to be afraid to go like that. I, too, was afraid, for her and for us.

A few days earlier in the hospital, during the last chemotherapy, as her nausea and pain were about to lock step one more time, I had summoned the courage to flag Dr. Burns and ask him a question. I caught up with him as he made his way down the hospital corridor, fresh from one of his Hi-how-are-you, walk-out-on-the-answer visits to my mother. The Indian resident, the Chinese resident, and the rabbinical intern surrounding him stared at me in unison. It was like stepping in front of a parade at the United Nations.

"Dr. Burns? I wonder if I could talk to you for a minute? My mother is in pretty bad shape. She hardly eats anymore, you know—did . . . did you know she can't keep food down?—and the pain doesn't seem to stop and I guess I just want to make sure there's a good chance that the chemotherapy will make her feel better. That's what I care about now and I think that's what she cares about—not to have her life prolonged, at this point, just to—to stop *suffering* . . ." My voice had gotten louder than I meant it to. I felt as if I had just sung an entire song off-key.

"Well, they usually feel better after a few treatments," he said, his eyes fixed in the usual place, on the floor.

"You mean because the chemotherapy shrinks the tumor, I know. But what if it doesn't? What if the tumor keeps growing and spreads and—"

"Well, when that happens they usually go pretty fast."

"How fast?"

"Oh, I've seen them go in a couple of weeks."

Oh, how I hate him and his *they/them* locution and his eyes on the floor, but at least, I thought, I've got it now. I think I've got it. The chemotherapy *maybe* makes the tumor shrink. This *maybe* makes her more comfortable. But if it doesn't, the cancer goes berserk and she dies fast. At least that.

The conversation with Dr. Burns was held at my mother's directive. "Please, sweetheart, talk to him," she had said. "Find out what's going on. I don't have the strength to ask him. He's got so many patients and I can't ever ask the questions fast enough."

When I walked back into her room she hadn't yet succumbed to the Thorazine, and although she was nauseous, the really bad, throwing-up nausea hadn't begun. She asked me what Dr. Burns had said, and since she rarely asked questions, I decided she must want to know. So I told her, softening it only a little.

"He said the chemotherapy would probably work, but . . ." I swallowed. "If it doesn't you'll . . . it'll spread very fast and it'll be over . . . fast."

She nodded slowly. Then she turned her head toward the window and sighed. "Oh, I hope so," she whispered. "I'd feel a lot better if I knew that were true."

12

chapter

August 30. Just as I began to think she'd never recover from the second chemotherapy (another four to go if Burns had his way), she more or less did. She ate very little, but she ate. She had pain still, but a higher dosage of medication seemed to be checking it. There were only two and a half weeks before they'd hit her again, but meanwhile she seemed to be holding.

So after a lot of back and forth about it (booking, canceling, rebooking), Ed and I decided to give ourselves a little break and go to the Berkshires for a week.

It didn't quite work. The distance between my mother and us was not great—a hundred miles or so—but it gave me a constant feeling of unease, and I did not trust her perky responses to our telephone calls. To my surprise, however, when we did return home at the end of the week, she seemed in as good shape as when we left, maybe even better. For that reason I felt fairly calm about the television assignment that was to take me out of town again the following week.

Besides, she wasn't exactly alone. Shany came almost every day; Ed was across town; her friend Rose lived around the corner; favorite niece Elaine didn't live in the city, but all anyone had to do was dial her number and she'd be at my mother's door with a trayful (more than my mother could eat in a year) of her heavenly noodle pudding. And since the chemotherapy had started up again, there was also a housekeeper we had found through the hospital who came in a few mornings a week. Although now my mother wanted to let her go.

"Don't you like Harriet?" I asked her on the phone.

"Of course I like her. She's the sweetest woman I ever met. She's got three children. All three she put through college. One is—"

"So why do you want to get rid of her?"

"Because I don't need anybody here."

"Is it the money?"

"Please! It's not the money." Of course it was. "Shany's here almost every afternoon, you know. I don't need her either. But she insists on coming."

That evening, I had a surprise call from Shany's son, Steven, who lives in Washington, D.C.

"I'm worried about my mother," he said.

"*Your* mother? What do you mean?"

"We saw her last week and she looks terrible. She's exhausted. She's spending too much time with your mother. You have to get a professional person to come in. It's too much for my mother."

I was stunned, and just a little put out. "Your mother's

been great, Steven, but a housekeeper *has* been coming in." I decided not to mention that she would no longer be coming in. "I really don't think your mother's been doing heavy housework or preparing gourmet meals."

"There's more to do than you probably realize. Your mother is very, very sick. She needs someone full-time to take care of her."

"She doesn't want anyone! I just had a fight with her about it this morning. She doesn't even want your mother there as often as she's been coming."

"My mother won't stop coming unless you get someone. I know her."

"Steven, I can't force my mother—"

"Well, I think you should. I think it's come to that."

He was right of course. I knew he was right as soon as we hung up, particularly in view of the fact that I was going off on a story the next day. I looked at the clock: eight-fifteen P.M. Ed had a late class. I called my mother and told her I was coming over.

"Shany looks tired," I said, following the line I had planned on the walk crosstown. "I think we should hire Harriet to come over here every day, just for a few weeks until you're stronger."

My mother was lying down. She had her little white cap on. If only, I thought, cisplatin did to her cancer what it does to her hair.

"I don't want her here every day. I already told you I don't want her here at all." She sounded annoyed. "It's a small apartment. I like her, but she talks a lot."

"What about getting Pearl? I'm sure she works in people's houses sometimes."

"Pearl? I don't need a nurse! What *is* all this?"

It was going to be harder than I thought. I didn't want to tell her about Steven's call. I didn't want her feeling guilty about Shany, and I didn't want Shany finding out about the call either. All that would accomplish would be to get Shany angry at Steven.

"It just sounds to me as if you need a little more help. I'm going out of town tomorrow and I'd feel better if someone was here."

"Shany is here."

Mother, I thought, how can you be this sick and this stubborn? But I knew what she was doing. She was simply trying to hold on to the person she used to be, the person in charge. She felt that person slipping and she wasn't about to let go. Not yet.

"What are all these pills?" I suddenly noticed about six or seven vials on her bed table, along with a couple of large bottles of over-the-counter stomach settlers.

"They're my pills," she said as if I were the enemy.

"I didn't realize you were taking so many different kinds." I picked up one of the vials. "Tylenol No. 3— that's with codeine, right?—for when you have pain."

"When *don't* I have pain?"

"I thought the pain was better."

She shrugged. "It's better when I don't eat."

I picked up another bottle. "Reglan. That's what they gave you in the hospital for nausea last time. Are you . . . you're not still nauseous are you?"

"Not really, once in a while. I take it before I eat. Dr. Goldman said it would help the food go down."

"Does it?"

She shrugged. "What is this? A third degree?"

"I just want to know what all this stuff is. Dalmane. What's that for?"

She sighed. "That's my favorite. It puts me to sleep."

"Does it work?"

"For a few hours."

"What did you eat today?"

"I ate."

"What? What did you have for breakfast?"

Another sigh. "An English muffin."

"A whole one?" She shook her head. "Half?"

"Almost half."

"What for lunch?"

"I didn't feel right today. I skipped lunch."

"What about dinner?"

"Shany fixed me some soup. I shouldn't have had it. Ever since that soup I've had a pain."

"Does Dr. Goldman know how little you're eating?"

"I told him."

"And?"

"He said to eat that liquid protein. I've got it in the refrigerator."

"Are you eating it?"

"I can't eat it. It's disgusting."

"Did you tell him."

"Of course not."

"What do you mean, 'of course not'?"

"I'm not going to tell him something he tells me to eat is disgusting."

"Mother, you shouldn't worry about being polite with Dr. Goldman! He would certainly want to know if you're not eating what he told you to eat, particularly if you're not eating anything else!"

"There's nothing they can give me to eat."

"But that's . . . you can't not eat!"

She shrugged. "I'm tired. Why don't you go home."

I'm tired. Why don't you go home. My mother had never said that to me before. "*You're* tired, go home," but never "I'm tired, go home." This was the new sick person speaking. I looked at her and she looked away from me.

I got up. Then I remembered Steven. "I know you're tired, but promise me you'll think about having someone come here during the day."

"I'm not going to promise because I don't want it."

"What about every other day?"

"Please!" she said and started to get up as if to say, if you won't leave, I will.

"Okay." I bent down to kiss her. "I hope you have a good night."

"I hope so too," said the sick person.

I was too much of a coward to call Steven and report my failure. As it turned out, however, I didn't have to call him because in two days she was getting all the full-time help he had said she needed. In two days she was back in the hospital.

Before I left on my assignment I had called Dr. Goldman from the airport. He said not to worry about her not eating as long as she didn't stop drinking and get dehydrated. "The tumor is blocking part of the intestine," he explained. "This is why she can't eat and this is why she has trouble moving her bowels. Our job is to try to unblock her system so that both food and waste will pass through it. The chemotherapy should help and so should those various medications." Should, I thought, should. Meanwhile, my flight had begun to board.

My story (on child abuse) didn't pan out. The ex-abuser, who had promised on the phone to spill the beans, changed her mind. Normally I would have gone all out to reconvince her, but since my mother's illness I had stopped going all out for work. I performed my journalistic duties, but I performed them with the passion of a receptionist. I didn't even have the emotional energy to feel guilty about it.

With the story killed, I was back to New York in two days. By now my mother had stopped drinking. She was throwing up everything, even water, even sips of water. On September 14 Shany and I took her to the hospital. She didn't want to go; she was cranky with me, worse with Shany. As soon as they hooked her up to an IV (of liquid nourishment), she turned her head away from us and went to sleep. Shany and I looked at each other and tiptoed out.

"Go home, you look terrible," we said to each other in unison and then laughed—a shaky laugh followed by a hug. When we got to the street Shany lit a cigarette. We talked for a minute, then went our separate ways home.

The next morning Ed and I walked up to the hospital. The air was moist and fresh and the shoppers hadn't yet invaded Fifth Avenue, so we took long strides and did a lot of inhaling. This is not one of those Sundays of two years ago, or even two months ago, I kept reminding myself. This is not a chemotherapy weekend. Calm down. But as we faced the hospital building and pushed through the revolving doors into the lobby, my stomach went on alert.

"I'll go first," I said to Ed when we got upstairs. With the usual grim expectations, I walked into her room. It took a full few seconds for my eyes and my brain to absorb what I saw.

Three, no, four fat people surrounded the bed of my mother's roommate. They were laughing. My mother was laughing too.

"Hi, sweetheart," she said in the voice of the person she used to be. Then to the others, "This is my Betts. And this is—let's see—this is Mrs. Hamburg and Mr. Hamburg and—oh, forgive me, dear, I'm so bad with names—"

"Estelle," said a fat girl with a basket of fruit on her lap.

"Marvin," said a sweet-faced fat boy parked on the foot of the bed.

I said hello and walked past them, with difficulty, to my mother's bed. "Hi," I said, kissing her on the cheek. "I guess it's all right for Ed to come in."

"You mean you've got my son standing out in the hallway?"

"It's not snowing out there, Mother," I said on my way to summoning Ed.

"This is my wonderful son-in-law," said my mother as Ed walked in, gaping. "I shouldn't say son-in-law because he is really my son."

Ed nodded at the assemblage and bent down to kiss her. "Hi, Ida. Gee, what are they giving you in that IV?"

"What do you mean?" she said, missing the joke the way she used to.

"You seem so much better," Ed said. "Like about two hundred percent better."

"Oh. Yeah, I guess so. Oh, are you leaving?" she said, looking past us toward the other half of the room. The party seemed to be breaking up.

"We're going to let Mom have a nap," said Marvin. "Nice to meet you!" he called and they all lumbered out.

My mother signaled us with her finger to come closer. "Hysterectomy," she said, nodding her head in the direction of the other bed. "They're lovely people. The younger daughter's having a hard time. She wants to marry a man twice her age. The son is in medical school. A lovely boy, *lovely* . . ."

I looked at Ed. Ed looked at me. And my mother continued the history of the Hamburgs.

"She was getting dehydrated and now she's not anymore," Dr. Goldman said later when I asked him what accounted for the change.

"But she doesn't even seem to have any more pain! I'm not complaining, you understand. I'm just confused. The cancer's still there, isn't it?"

"The cancer's still there. We'll do some scans tomorrow. We should know more after that. But, you know, there are bound to be ups and downs with this thing. You think someone is declining, and they shoot up. But I have to tell you, they can just as rapidly shoot down."

Oh, Dr. Goldman, I listened to your words that day, but I should have written them down and repeated them each day like the catechism. Of all warnings that the families of sick people need to heed, the one that goes *Don't expect logic* merits the most scholarly attention. Don't expect a good turn to get better. Don't even expect a bad turn to get worse. Don't expect. But one does, and in spite of the doctor's words, I thought the good turn she had taken might extend for a bit. But no.

Not that she crashed. It was more of a crumble than a crash, the sort of crumble, however, that adds up to a crash.

In the hospital they gave her something to get her bowels going. But then she began having the opposite problem. Her bowels were functioning, but crazily, unpredictably. Adding to her difficulty was the location of the bathroom—on the other side of the room next to Mrs. Hamburg's bed and surrounded, usually, by all of the other Hamburgs.

When I visited her the next day I found her near tears. "I can't control myself," she whispered, looking over at Mrs. Hamburg, who was sleeping soundly. "I can't always make it to the bathroom in time! It's so embarrassing with all of those people. I have to walk past them and sometimes one of them is in the bathroom and—it's awful. I don't know what to do!"

This, I thought, we don't need. "I'll be right back," I told her and started to walk out.

She called me back. "What are you going to do? Please, Betty," she stage-whispered, "don't complain about those people. They're lovely people. It's not their fault."

"Don't worry. That's not what I had in mind at all. It's a nursing problem is what it is. I'm just going to speak to Irish to see if there's something they can do for you."

"No, please don't bother the nurses. I'm enough trouble already. They had to change my bed three times today. And they couldn't be sweeter about it. What more can they do?"

"I don't know, but look, I'll just ask. There's got to be something."

And there was. Something very simple—a commode, a portable toilet that could be put up right next to the bed.

However—the Chinese probably have a proverb for this—in a hospital, between agreeing on a simple solution and putting that solution into effect there often exists a yawning chasm. Irish had the day off, so I asked another nurse about the commode. She told me she would get it, but that it was on another floor. Fine. Except she forgot. I reminded her. "Oh, *right!*" she said. She forgot again. This time, however, she gave a reason; she was too busy. Finally, two days later, they pushed the thing into the room. A perfect solution it was not, but at least in an emergency she could pull the curtain and get to the commode a lot faster than she could get to the bathroom, and she wouldn't have to trip over her roommate's entire family on the way.

Alvin had been wanting to visit my mother and she had been putting him off. The same night the commode arrived, he called me at home.

"Tell her I don't care what she looks like. And I won't stay long. I'll just say hello and good-bye. And if she feels really rotten I'll say hello and good-bye real fast."

"Actually, she's a little better. At least there's no pain right now. I'll talk to her."

I talked to her. Still she balked. "Look at me," she said pointing to her white cap. "And I'm worried about that other problem too."

"He's seen you before without hair," I said, ignoring the second problem.

"Before, I wore a wig."

"So wear a wig now."

"I can't. It looks funny in a hospital bed to wear a wig."

"It doesn't look funny. But your white cap doesn't look funny either. It looks sweet. Besides, do you think Alvin cares what you look like? Give him a little credit, will you? It's really not kind of you to shut him out this way. Hasn't he—"

"All right, all right," she said. "Let him come."

And the next day he did. By the time I stopped in later that evening, Alvin had been and gone. The instant I saw her face I knew something bad had happened. She was lying on her back, her arms under the covers as if she were bound, staring at the wall. Her lips looked dry and white. When I came in, she hardly turned her head.

"What's wrong?" I asked her, pulling up a chair next to the bed. No answer. "Mother, what's wrong? Please tell me."

She shook her head and her lip began to quiver. I took her hand and felt my own lip go. More than anything, it was the shock of seeing her cry. As emotional as she was, my mother didn't cry, at least not in front of me. My father's funeral was the only exception I could think of. We had stood together, my arm around her shoulders, and I had felt her tremble. Now that my mind had traveled back there again, I remembered not wanting to look at her face. I didn't want to look now either.

"What is it?" I said again, turning to see if we had an audience. But Mrs. Hamburg was alone and asleep.

My mother pressed her lips together and shook her head. One tear spilled out of her eye and, like a small, lost vehicle, rolled down her cheek and disappeared behind her cap.

"I've never been so humiliated," she said in a hoarse voice.

"What happened?"

"Alvin."

"What did Alvin do?"

"It isn't what Alvin did. It's what I did." She nodded her head in the direction of Mrs. Hamburg. "She had her whole family here when he came, so we went to the visitors' room down the hall. I thought it would be more private there." Her eyes were on me now, enlarged by their sorrow, like a child reporting to her mother something terrible that had happened at school that day. "I had on the pretty robe you gave me, the one with the flowers." She stopped for a moment and again pressed her lips together. Then she went on. "We were talking and he was saying all those things about wanting to see me more and not caring how I look, and then . . . all of a sudden I had to go to the bathroom . . . and I said excuse me and got up, and when I got there I looked at the back of my robe and it was soiled, and I looked down at the floor and I had . . . left spots on the floor, and I probably smelled, too . . . and I'm sure he saw. He must have seen." She wasn't crying anymore, but she looked as miserable as a person who is not crying can look.

"I am so humiliated," she said slowly, turning her head

toward the window. "I am so humiliated. I don't ever want to see him again. I never want to see him again. I have no control any more. It's not . . . I can't . . ."

If only a note would drop from heaven telling me what to say.

"Mother, you're . . . I know how you feel, but really it doesn't matter as much as you think. It certainly doesn't matter to Alvin. It's just your body doing crazy things. It's not *you*, mother, it's not you. Try to think . . . please, Mother, don't look so miserable . . ." I kissed her hand and held it against my cheek. It was cool and soft. "Maybe Alvin didn't even notice. Did you think of that?" I babbled on, but the conversation was over and I knew it. I might as well have been talking to myself.

"I'm sorry," she said finally in a dead voice. "Let's change the subject," and she did. But she never was quite the same after that. And though they continued to speak on the phone, she never did see Alvin again.

13

chapter

September 23. She was due for another chemo, but they decided she couldn't take it and sent her home to "get a little stronger." So explained Dr. Goldman. I would have guessed that she'd be relieved at not having to face chemotherapy. I was wrong. She saw it, correctly, as a sign that she was too ill for it to work.

"That's some medicine," she said, noting the irony. "You have to be healthy before they can give it to you."

Dr. Burns had come by the previous evening. My mother gave him one of her little girl smiles and said, "I guess you're giving up on me."

He responded on cue: "Not at all. Not at all." Not at all convincing, I thought and asked myself a pointless question that I had asked myself before: Can you teach a doctor what Dr. Burns doesn't know how to do? Maybe, came the pointless answer, if he thought he needed to learn it. But if that were the case, he probably would have learned it long ago.

After he left she looked as blue as I'd seen her since Alvin's visit the week before. "He's giving up on me," she said and turned her face toward the window.

The next day she kissed Mrs. Hamburg good-bye and they exchanged good wishes in what sounded like a Hebrew prayer. "May you always be well," said my mother. We took her home unarmed, for the first time, with a plastic dish.

I hired a new housekeeper to come each morning, a nice Haitian lady with enough problems, I was sure, to keep my mother's interest. My mother said nothing when I told her; she knew it had to be. Both Shany and I were going to be out of town for a few days. Shany had a trip planned to visit Steven and his family in Washington, and I was off to Norfolk, Virginia, to pick up on the child abuse story I'd begun before my mother's last hospitalization. We both felt uneasy about going, but my mother insisted she'd be fine. She didn't really need the housekeeper, she said, but she was willing to humor us.

I left Monday morning. When I called Monday evening, she sounded all right but far away in a way that had nothing to do with geography. She mentioned that her friend Rose had come by. "Rose has so much energy," my mother said with a weak laugh. "It made me tired just to look at her."

The next day in Norfolk, I fixed my mind on the child abuse story. The producer and I had talked our way into covering a meeting of Parents Anonymous, a group patterned, as the name suggests, after Alcoholics Anonymous for child abusers who want to change their ways. After the session I interviewed one woman who hadn't said much during the meeting but whose face said a lot. I supposed she was young, although you'd never have described her that way. Her face was puffy, her eyes were slits, and her hair was pulled back so tight it looked as if it hurt.

She answered immediately when I asked her what kind of mother she was. "Rotten," she said, and laughed.

"What do you mean?"

"I used to treat my oldest boy like the way my mom treated me."

"What does that mean?"

"I beat the shit out of him."

If I was looking for distraction, I had found it. And although I didn't know it and surely wouldn't have admitted it, I was looking for distraction. By now my mother's disease—no fault of hers or mine or anyone else's—had taken over my life. Of course it had. When someone you love gets very sick that's simply what happens. It probably even happens when someone gets very sick whom you're supposed to love and *don't* particularly. Disease may score a direct hit on only one member of a family, but shrapnel tears the flesh of the others. And as I had learned, there was no quick way out of the war zone.

In a sense I didn't want out of the war zone. My mother's disease and my mother had become one, and I didn't want to get away from my mother. And yet I did. Oh, how I did. And child abuse worked as a temporary escape the way an afternoon movie wouldn't have, because child abuse wasn't any fun. No fun equaled no guilt. How could I feel guilty for deserting my mother for a Serious Social Problem?

So I leapt through the fence and burrowed into the case of the woman who beat the shit out of her kid. I interviewed her until we were both exhausted, and I interviewed others who weren't as spicy, but never mind. The camera kept rolling and I kept digging and not until the next morning, when the sunlight gently seeped through the curtains in my hotel room in Norfolk, Virginia, did I wake up and remember that I had a sick mother in New York. My little vacation was over.

I called her and got a busy signal, which I knew was either a good sign or a bad sign—a good sign if it meant she was talking to someone, a bad sign if she had taken the receiver off the hook. She took it off—usually not for long—when she felt too sick to talk to anyone.

We were to leave Norfolk early and fly to Washington, where we planned to screen and edit the tape we had shot. I tried calling my mother from the airport in Norfolk. The line was still busy. I tried again when we landed in Washington. Busy.

We arrived at the ABC office in Washington at about noon. The producer, heading straight for the editing room, called back that she didn't need me right away. I dropped my overnight bag on the floor and picked up a phone on one of the empty desks in the newsroom. Busy. I sat down at the desk and tried to think. No one was around yet—the "Nightline" staff didn't get in until around three—so I could think out loud, as I do sometimes. Talking to yourself is supposed to be what crazy people do, but doing it always makes me feel less crazy.

"She fell asleep," I said as the wire copy machines ticked in the background. "She fell asleep and she forgot about the phone. But where's Florence [the housekeeper]? If the phone was off the hook, surely she would notice. Maybe Florence isn't there. She only works mornings. Maybe she's already left. But what about before she left? Why didn't she notice it then? Unless my mother told her she wanted the phone off the hook. But ..." I dialed the number again. Busy.

"It's out of order," I said and the sound of my voice—a shade louder now—made me believe it. The trouble is, I thought, there's no way to find out if it's out of order. I knew from past experience that a phone off the hook and a phone out of order registered the same. I dialed the operator and asked her to check anyway. No success.

I called Ed. He had a class in five minutes, he said, but after the class he'd go up to her apartment. We hung up and I dialed my mother's number again. "Busy," I said out loud. I got up. I sat down. I had a new idea. I dialed information. My mother's building had a telephone in the lobby, which I knew had an outside line because I had seen the doorman use it. It just might be listed, I thought. It was. As the number rang I shut my eyes and hoped it would be the man I knew.

"John?" I said when a voice answered.

"Yes?"

"John, this is Betty Rollin, Mrs. Rollin's daughter?"

"Oh yes. What can I do for you?"

"Well, I have a favor to ask you. I'm out of town right now and—you know my mother's been sick—and she seems to have the phone off the hook, and—you didn't see her go out or anything did you?"

"No ma'am, I didn't see her. I haven't seen your mother in quite a while now."

"In that case would you please try calling her on the house phone, and when—if—she answers, tell her to put her phone on the hook because I'm trying to call her, okay?"

"Okay, sure."

Five dollars, I thought. No, ten dollars. As soon as I get back to New York I'll give him ten dollars. "Thanks so much, John. I'll hang up now and try to call her in a few minutes."

I made myself wait three minutes on the clock. Then I

dialed. The phone was ringing. Thank God. Then it stopped. A voice said hello, but it was not my mother's voice. I knew my mother's voice and this voice was high and breathy, not her voice at all. But I got confused because suddenly I heard the voice say "Hello, sweetheart."

"Mother?"

"Yes . . . Shorry 'bout the phone . . . off the hook . . . very shorry . . ." She sounded drunk.

"Mother, what's the matter?" Calm, I ordered myself. *Be calm.*

"Oh jush shleeping . . . can't . . . what time? What time is it?"

"It's after one o'clock. What's the matter. You sound strange. What is it? Are you alone? Where's Florence?"

"Florensh? Dunno where ish she. She wen' home, I think she wen' home. What . . . day is it?"

"Mother, listen to me. Don't do anything, okay? Just stay in bed and I'll be there as soon as I can. Don't try to get up or anything, okay? And don't take any pills. Is that it? Did you take too much medication?"

"Medicashun?"

"Okay, never mind. I'll be there as soon as I can."

I looked at the clock as I hung up. One-fifteen. I could get a two o'clock shuttle. That meant I'd get to New York at about three, to my mother's at three-thirty. Too late. Ed. No, Ed was still in his class. Besides, he's way downtown. Rose, I thought, I'll get my mother's friend Rose. Rose lives only a block away. Please let information have her number. Please let Rose be home. Please . . .

"Rose?"

"Yes?"

Could she, I asked her, possibly get over to my mother's right away? Yes, she said, of course.

"And I'll be there as soon as I can."

"Not to worry," she said.

Oh thank you, Rose, thank you. I hoisted my overnight bag over my shoulder and on my way out nearly collided with the producer. "Oh!" she said, startled. "I was just coming to get you!" Pushing for the elevator, I apologized and explained hurriedly why I had to go.

"Go," she said at once. "We can do this any time."

On the way down I wondered why I didn't feel guilty or worried about my job. I'll do that later, I thought, as the elevator landed. Then I bolted for a taxi.

As soon as Rose opened the door it hit me—the smell. It was revolting and powerful, and there was no doubt about what it was. My mother's bowels must have exploded. Why hadn't Rose opened a window? But as I moved into the apartment I saw the curtain flapping. She *had* opened the window.

I walked into the bedroom and stopped. My mother lay on the bed with the covers pulled down. Her nightgown was twisted around her body, her head turned toward the wall. Her head was bald. I knew that of course, but since she always wore her little cap, I hadn't seen her that way since the first round of chemotherapy two years ago. When she rolled her head around to look at me I gasped. Her eyelids were half shut; her face was yellow. She looked dead.

Slowly, I came nearer. The sheets were smeared with feces, as was her nightgown. The stench packed my nostrils. I felt if I came any nearer, there wouldn't be any air to breathe at all. I reached my arms out to her. Mother, I sobbed inside, oh Mother, Mother, Mother.

I cleaned her up—she was as limp and docile as a sweet-natured drunk—and after an hour or so, with Rose's help, I pieced together what had happened. During the night she had had a lot of pain accompanied by violent diarrhea, and she had simply overmedicated herself. Florence, the housekeeper, had probably left at noon as she usually did. (To give her the benefit of the doubt we assumed, Rose and I, that Florence left my mother sleeping and not in the state Rose found her in.)

As soon as Rose arrived, she tried to find out what doctor to call, but my mother wasn't coherent enough to tell her. Finally Rose managed to find the number and get Dr. Goldman on the phone. He asked to speak to my mother directly, then again to Rose. He told her that my mother's disorientation did not seem extreme enough to warrant an emergency admittance to the hospital, but that he was concerned about dehydration (as a result of the diarrhea) and would, therefore, try to arrange for an admittance the next day.

Rose and I had this conversation in whispers in the living room after my mother had fallen asleep. Rose seemed very shaken, and no wonder. I looked at my mother's friend, lined in the face and near my mother's age, but young and bright in the eyes like my mother—like my mother used to be. Dear Rose, in her bright dress and Mexican shawl, sitting on the edge of the sofa, her hands on her knees. Before today, it occurred to me, she probably had never seen my mother without makeup. She was talking fast now, still in a whisper, about something that had happened during the call to Dr. Goldman. Her back had been turned, and when she turned toward her again she saw that my mother had dropped to the floor. Frightened, Rose ran to her, only to find that my mother had a towel in her hand which she was pushing around the carpet, trying to wipe up the mess she had made. "Don' look," she said to Rose with tears in her eyes. "Please don' look."

The next day she was back in the hospital, back on the IV, back in the role of the withering plant in need of water. As usual, after she got it, she perked up. The yellowness in the hollows of her cheeks faded, her eyes cleared, the diarrhea subsided. Still, she did not revive the way she had in the past. It was as if something in her root had dried permanently. The word *chemotherapy*, I noticed—and so, I knew, did she—had stopped coming up in conversations with the doctors. It was strange to think how much it would have cheered us if it had.

Before I left the hospital that day she asked me a question: "This is how it's going to be from now on, isn't it?"

I couldn't answer because the answer, we both knew, was yes. Yes, and worse.

14

chapter

We were about to have another problem. My mother had reached the stage of needing constant care or, at least, constant monitoring. In the hospital she got it. In the hospital she wouldn't overdose on medication because nurses were around to make sure she didn't. In the hospital she wouldn't dehydrate because in the hospital an IV was always a stab in the vein away. The problem was she couldn't stay in the hospital.

Dr. Goldman had warned me about this. Once my mother went off the IV, and now that resuming chemotherapy sounded more and more unlikely, she did not *need* to be hospitalized. Yes, there were the continuing effects of her malignancy—the frequent eruptions and blockages of her bowels, her ongoing inability to digest food, and her pain, all of which would undoubtedly worsen. Suffering was surely in store. Still, this was not suffering requiring hospitalization, not right now anyway, and so she would be asked to leave.

In case I didn't get the picture, a social worker came by the next day to draw it for me. I felt as though I were being served with a summons. She caught me as I left my mother's room to go to the bathroom.

"Miss Rollin?"

"Yes."

"May I speak to you for a moment?"

I had no reason to hate her as I immediately did. She didn't know I was on my way to the bathroom and she was just, as they say, doing her job. But as she stood there with her clipboard and her twenty-seven-year-old face and a barrette in her straight, squeaky clean hair, speaking to me in administrativese ("I'm afraid I must inform you that given your mother's present condition . . ."), telling me what I didn't want to hear at a moment I particularly didn't want to hear it, I stood there, fixed under the fluorescent light in the hospital corridor, hating her with all my heart.

"Have you considered the possibility of a nursing home facility?" she asked with a perky tilt of her head.

"Please!" I said in my mother's voice. "You'll have to excuse me. I have to go to the bathroom."

But she caught me on the return trip, deftly rewinding her nursing home tape and playing it again. "There are many fine nursing home facilities in the city. Most of them, unfortunately, have a waiting list, but—"

"Miss . . ." I squinted at the nameplate on her lapel, "Brown. I am not about to send my mother to a nursing home."

But Miss Brown pressed her index finger on the play button and the tape continued. Again, I can't blame her.

She must have heard family members being uppity about nursing homes before, only to have them change their tune after becoming acquainted with a few realities, like the cost of home care. At that time, it cost approximately $350 each day for registered nurses around the clock, somewhat less for licensed practical nurses, and about $175 for nurse's aides—expenses uninsured by most policies.

I admit I was stunned. And my mother, I knew, would be worse than stunned. She was so proud of the money she had saved. She'd probably rather die, literally, than spend it this way. Still, we were lucky; we had a choice. We could, in fact, be uppity about a nursing home. My mother had some money. I had some money. We'd feel this, but it wouldn't break us. Besides, we didn't need nurses. Aides would be fine. Perhaps we could get Pearl again. She'd come to the house. I knew she would.

I wondered whether to tell my mother the truth about all of this. I had become less and less of a purist about truth. I leaned toward it, but not automatically. Truth had become too harsh lately for automatic dissemination. I decided to tell it to her this time, though—if she asked. For one thing, nursing fees were something she could easily check.

She didn't react the way I thought she would. I expected her to hit the hospital ceiling, but she didn't come close. She just lay there with her new, sad eyes and her turned-down mouth and murmured, "I don't need anybody, I don't need anybody." But she knew she did, I could tell by the way she said it. So I didn't argue. I just stroked her forehead and told her I'd try to get Pearl. She turned her head and looked out the window.

"This is so silly," she said in a flat voice.

I sat down on the bed and tried to see her face. "What's silly?"

"My life now."

"What do you mean?" I said, hedging. I knew very well what she meant.

She turned toward me and looked straight in my eyes. "It doesn't make sense anymore. My life is over. It's time to go. Why can't I go?" She said this as if she were asking permission to leave the room.

A nurse came in with a cup of juice and a pill. My mother sat up and took it without a word. The nurse left and my mother looked at me again. "Why can't they give me a pill that would end it?"

"They can't do that," I said, looking at the bed covers.

"Why can't they?"

"It's against the law."

"It shouldn't be. If a person wants to go, they should help." Her lips were tight. She held the edges of the sheets in her fists as if they were reins. "What's the point of trapping you in life if you don't want it?" she said, trying to find my eyes which were still pinned on the bed. "It's cruel. They don't care. They don't care what a person really wants. They care about their profession, not the people they practice it on. Look at Dr. Burns. He comes in—he was here this morning—he goes out. He tells me about the ball game. He can't help me any more, so he tells me about the ball game. I said to him, 'Dr. Burns,' I said, 'my life is over. There's no point in it anymore. Why can't you give me a pill?' He looks at the floor, like he's embarrassed. 'Now Ida,' he says, 'that's no way to talk.' And then he gets out of here. I never saw him leave so fast!"

I listened to her. I did listen, but I didn't hear. Or like Dr. Burns (what new alliance was this? Dr. Burns and I against my mother?), I didn't want to hear. "You'll feel better when we get you home," I said. Miraculously, my nose didn't grow.

"No I won't. How can I feel better if I know you're spending all that money on nurses?"

"It's not my money. It's yours."

"That's silly and you know it. My money is your money. What do you think Daddy and I saved for all those years, for nurses? To keep me alive when I don't want to be kept alive?"

"Mother, you're lucky you have the money. Okay, *we're* lucky *we* have it. It means we can afford to take care of you. It means you don't have to . . ." I stopped. She doesn't need to hear that, I thought. Not with everything else that's going on in her head right now. She doesn't need to hear how things could be worse.

As soon as I got her home the next day, we had a fight about hiring an overnight aide. Pearl said she'd work the day shift, from eight A.M. to eight P.M., and she had a friend who would cover the other twelve hours. "Isn't that great?" I said to my mother. "If she's Pearl's friend she must be nice."

"What's great about it? I don't want anyone overnight. Overnight I just sleep. I don't need someone sitting here looking at me while I sleep."

"Mother, please . . ."

"It's silly and I don't want it." She sighed. "What I want is for it to be over."

Oh God, I thought, not that again.

Finally I resorted to an old trick. I told her if she didn't have someone there at night, I'd worry and lose sleep. It worked. Silently she acquiesced. We all went limp with relief, but for me it was a joyless win. What I had done, I knew, was force her to end her life as an adult. You can't be alone, I had said to her. You need to be watched. You need care, you need help. You're not capable anymore. You're a baby.

An old baby.

It had to be done. We both knew that. But it made her eyes so liquid and mournful that sometimes I couldn't look at them. There was no way to comfort her either, no way to say, "It'll pass." We both knew it wouldn't.

Meanwhile we had solved a part of the problem by hiring aides, but not the whole problem. Aides don't practice medicine. Therefore my mother had no medical attention, except what we could get on the telephone from Dr. Goldman. Dr. Burns, meanwhile, like a teacher from last year's grade, had totally faded from the picture. My mother had nothing like the emotional fix on Dr. Goldman she had had on Dr. Burns, but she liked Goldman and so did I. He had no magical solutions, but he was approachable, honest, sympathetic, and the rest of it. "The rest of it," however, did not include house calls. So we were in a peculiar bind. The only way my mother could be seen by a doctor was to be hospitalized, but it had been determined that she didn't need hospitalization. Goldman would have seen her in his office, but she was no longer capable of making that kind of excursion.

She could just about make it to the bathroom, and she needed help to do that. In addition to her general weakness, her legs had recently given out. They buckled under her, as if to say, this body isn't worth holding up anymore. And two days after her last return home, her system stopped working again. She couldn't eat, she could barely drink, and once again she was unable to move her bowels.

When I reported this on the telephone to Dr. Goldman, he sighed and prescribed suppositories. We were about to end the conversation when I heard myself ask a question I hadn't planned to ask. It might have had something to do with his sigh, which I heard, not as a professional sound, but as a helpless, human one. I recognized it I suppose, because I held that sigh in my own lungs, but it hadn't broken yet. So I asked the question I had no right to ask: How much longer? He said he didn't know, but I pressed him to guess.

"It could be several weeks. It could be several months," he said. "More likely several months."

"Could it be a year?"

"I doubt that. No."

When we hung up I did something I hadn't done for a while. I sat down on the edge of my bed, and I covered my face with my hands and cried. It was a good cry, and it felt terrible and wonderful the way good cries do. To this day I'm not sure whether I was crying because my mother was going to live or because she was going to die. Part of me wanted her to die, so "several months" sounded like a long time, given what she was going through and that it could only get worse. And part of me couldn't bear for her to die, and to that part "several months" sounded like tomorrow. I hated both choices and what I hated most of all was knowing they were not choices.

That's what frightened me. And that's what frightened her, especially when she thought about my mother-in-law, Marian, about Marian trying to starve, trying to die, and about how long it took, how very long. It isn't that she talked about it so much, but now and then it bobbed up in a conversation that was about something else altogether. So I knew it was on her mind. I knew she was frightened about what was in store.

I blew my nose, went into the bathroom, and splashed my face with cold water. Then I sat down again and tried to get myself back on the planning track. There had to be something better than nurse's aides and telephone calls to Goldman, and of course I knew exactly what it was—Hospice. Hospice would know how to keep my mother comfortable at home. With Hospice she would have visits from nurses and, when necessary, from doctors. And at least some of those services would be covered by Medicare (my mother would spark to that news). Thoughts about Hospice had crossed my mind before, but before they'd seemed premature. Now I knew they were not.

When I called, I found out that only one Hospice in New York offered home care and, not surprisingly, it was overbooked. They put her name on a waiting list. As I hung up the phone I tried to summon up thoughts Pollyanna: We're not desperate like some people, I recited silently, we have help, we're lucky we can afford it, etc., etc., all the while hating myself for not having planned ahead the way my mother would have.

My mother seemed to have hit it off with Pearl's friend, Belva. As soon as I met her I could see why. Belva was a Jamaican, ample and smooth-skinned, with the same face she must have had as a little girl, and a child's way of holding herself, head bowed and feet turned in. Her eyes were something else, however. Her eyes met mine directly, confidently. They were, I was happy to see, take-charge eyes.

She opened the door to my mother's apartment when I came by that evening, and in a soft Jamaican accent she introduced herself. I shook her hand and asked her to call me Betty, which I saw right away, by the uncomfortable smile that suddenly appeared on her face and the way her eyes dropped to her feet, was a mistake. Pearl had called me Betty from the start, but this woman had a more formal style—particularly, I guessed, in the company of white employers.

My mother's eyes were closed. I sat down on the armchair nearest to her bed and surveyed the collection of pills on her night table. Since Belva's arrival they were far more neatly arranged. Next to the pills was a folder, a kind of makeshift chart I had rigged up for the two women to follow. The page on top listed my mother's medication, what she was taking for what:

Tylenol No. 3 (fat bottle) contains codeine, one every 3 or 4 hours—for pain
Mylanta, best taken after meals—to settle stomach
Demerol, 50 mg—for pain
Reglan, one 4 times a day, ten minutes before eating (always)—for digestion and for nausea
Dalmane, one at bedtime—for sleep
Dulcolax suppository—for constipation

At the bottom of the sheet I had listed foods she might eat on those days she ate anything at all:

Breakfast (Reglan first): farina
Lunch: soup or yogurt or egg or ½ English muffin
Dinner: soup or egg

Clipped together on another set of pages, Belva and Pearl were keeping a record of my mother's intake, drugs on one side, food on the other. I glanced at—then read—the sheet Belva had begun the previous night.

Drugs	Food
11:25 P.M. one Dalmane	H_2O, ½ glass
12 midnight one Tylenol No. 3	
3 A.M. two Tylenol No. 3	H_2O, ½ glass
4:20 A.M. one-half Dalmane	H_2O, sip

5:30 A.M. threw up
8 A.M. threw up
9 A.M. Dulcolax suppository
[here, a change to Pearl's somewhat messier handwriting]
9:50 A.M.   farina, 1 tablespoon
10 A.M. Reglan
11:30 A.M. Tylenol No. 3 H_2O, ¼ glass
1:15 P.M. Reglan
2:45 P.M. Reglan
3:15 P.M. Mylanta
4:15 P.M. Dulcolax supposi-
    tory
4:30 P.M. Tylenol H_2O, ½ glass
4:40 P.M. Mylanta
4:50 P.M. vomited
5:45 P.M. Reglan
6:00 P.M.   soup, 2 tablespoons

As I looked up from the chart, my mother opened her
eyes. "Hello, sweetheart," she said in a whisper.

"Hi, Mother." I went to her and kissed her on the forehead. "Do you feel any better?"

She shrugged as if the query bored her; I now remembered it did. Just yesterday she had reported her difficulty
with the entire how-are-you line of questioning. "People
call and ask me how I am. What can I say? They want me
to say 'better' or something positive. Like Alvin. Every
day he calls and he asks me. I'm not going to lie, but what
can I say? That I'm worse? It's the truth, but I can't do
that to people."

I heard a sound from the kitchen. "I think Belva is fix-
ing something for you."

"Oh, I hope not," she sighed. "Every time I swallow
something I'm in trouble."

I sighed too. "Belva's nice," I whispered.

"She's not nice. She's wonderful," said my mother. She gestured for me to come nearer. "Very religious," she whispered. "She's a Seventh Baptist."

I smiled. "I thought you didn't like that."

She shook her head. "I don't like it when they try to convert me. She doesn't do that. She's an angel." Again she motioned me nearer. "Her son's in Jamaica; I think she's got trouble with him. Nothing about a husband. She's younger than she looks—about your age, I think. I told her it's not too late to find someone. I told her about how you just found Ed. I made it sound a little more recent than it was. She's a darling. She should be married. Maybe at her church, I told her, she could meet someone ..."

Belva interrupted us. "Would you like a little cold water, Mrs. Rollin? Or some tea?" Tactfully she let her voice precede her appearance at the door.

"No, darling," said my mother. "Maybe later." Belva nodded and retreated into the kitchen. My mother closed her eyes. I watched her and said nothing, hoping she'd fall asleep. But after only a minute or so she opened her eyes.

"I don't feel so great," she said. "I shouldn't have had that soup."

"Don't blame yourself. You only had two tablespoons. That's what the chart says."

"It's Shany's soup. She made it. I used to love it ..." She trailed off and closed her eyes again, only for a moment. "Maybe if I sit up," she said.

"That's a good idea," I said, not of course having any idea if it was a good idea or not. I helped her and for a moment she sat straight up in bed, very still, staring at the opposite wall.

Nausea—unaccompanied by vomiting—is not something you can see, but my mother's nausea I could see. I saw it in her eyes, on her mouth, in the slightly forward tilt of her head. I could almost feel it. I think I wanted to feel it, as if by feeling it I could absorb some of it.

She put her hand on her stomach. "Maybe if we walk to the window."

"Good!" I said with absurd enthusiasm and pulled the covers back. Her nightgown was above her knees, her short, chubby legs sticking straight out, toes touching like a child's. The sight of her legs and her chunky, white baby feet made me want to cry. I put my arm under her legs and moved them around to the side of the bed. "Sit for a minute first," I said, remembering what a nurse had told me once about getting up in stages to avoid dizziness.

She obeyed. Of course she obeyed. She would have obeyed a robot. She would have obeyed anything or anyone who sounded as if they had even the smallest notion of how to interrupt the waves of nausea now gathering momentum in her stomach and beginning to crest in her throat. So she sat, waiting for her next instruction. As she waited, her head fell to one side as if her neck were in a noose.

"Want to try it now?" I whispered. She nodded and I helped her up. We began to walk very, very slowly toward the living room.

"Do you want your slippers?"

She shook her head no. "Maybe if we walk to the window," she said again. She was fighting now.

"Good idea. Breathe deeply," I said—another tip from a nurse, useless, I knew. We got to the window and I shoved it open with my free hand and, leaning on me still, she inhaled and exhaled and, again, inhaled and exhaled.

"I'd like to sit down now," she whispered, so we sat, gingerly, on the edge of the sofa, as if it were illegal to be there. The sounds of traffic—of life, of healthy people—came through the open window. Side by side we sat dumbly and listened. I looked out at the sky. It was black.

My mother shut her eyes and took another deep breath.

"That's good," I said, "that's very good." She was losing and we both knew it. My eyes fell on the coffee table in front of us, at the assemblage of small objects that had been there for as long as I could remember, the same objects on the same coffee table in all of the different apartments and houses my mother had lived in. There was the cut glass candy dish, the cloisonné cigarette box and matching ashtray, and the most recent additions, Ed's books stacked next to mine—all the parts of my mother's road show—objects of display for guests who no longer came.

"I think," my mother said slowly, "I better go to the bathroom."

I held her under the arms as she got to her feet and we moved silently across the room. I knew better than to make any more coaching suggestions. The game was over.

She motioned me away when we reached the bathroom. Then Belva appeared as if by parachute and pushed open the bathroom door. The two of them went inside. I leaned against the wall and listened, first to the silence, then to the sound of my mother vomiting. Vomiting what? I wondered. She has nothing to vomit. I backed into her bedroom, sat down on the bed, and rubbed my eyes. There is no way to win this, I thought, no way at all.

They emerged from the bathroom, my mother in front, Belva holding her up from the back as if she were a broken marionette, speaking to her softly. "Almost there, Mrs. Rollin, a few more steps now, yes, that's good . . ." When they reached their destination, Belva lowered my mother onto the bed, cradled her knees and back, and, aiming just right for the middle of the bed, eased her down under the covers. Then she pulled the covers up, folded the sheet over the top of the blanket, and smoothed it, all the while making sounds of a spoken lullaby.

When my mother closed her eyes, Belva slipped back noiselessly into the kitchen, where on the counter, I had noticed earlier, she had a small, half-finished piece of embroidery and a religious pamphlet entitled "Themes of Faith and Salvation."

My mother slept for a while. When she woke up she said she felt better—not better enough to ingest anything, only better enough not to feel like throwing up again.

"Rose was here this morning," she said, too weak now to speak above a whisper. "She seemed so young to me, so lively. I looked at her and realized how far I've fallen." I pulled my chair closer to the bed and took her hand. "You know I love Rose, but the whole time she was here I kept wanting her to go so that I could sleep. It's the only relief I have now—sleep." Gently she took her hand out of mine and looked at me, her eyes wide and hard. "How am I going to get out of this?" she said. "Where's the door?"

Her eyes were too much for me. I looked down, but when I looked up they were still there. I think that's when I knew she was really asking me.

"I've had a wonderful life, but now it's over, or it should be. I'm not afraid to die but I am afraid of this illness, what it's doing to me. I'm not better. I'm worse. There's never any relief from it now. Nothing but nausea and this pain. The pain—it never stops. There won't be any more chemotherapy. There's no treatment anymore. Dr. Burns said when I reached this stage I'd go fast. But I'm not going; I can feel that. So what happens to me now? I know what happens. I'll die slowly." She paused, she coughed, but she kept her eyes on me. "I don't want that. I wouldn't mind if it killed me fast. Fast I wouldn't mind. Slow I mind." She stopped and at last she looked away. I laced my fingers and pressed my palms together. I thought that was the end of it, but she went on.

"Who does it benefit if I die slowly? If it benefits my children I'd be willing. If some good came to them, so I'd suffer a little. For my children I'd do that. Any mother would do that. But it's not going to do you any good. It's not going to do Ed any good. Just the opposite. Don't I see what I'm doing to you already? You haven't been this thin since you were in high school. There's no point in a slow death, none. I've never liked doing things with no point. I've got to end this."

She stopped. Now I was supposed to speak. My tongue was dry. "Mother," I said in a voice so low it was almost no voice at all, "what are you saying to me? I know it's been . . . I know you've had a really terrible twenty-four hours, forty hours. I know, I read the chart. But some days aren't so bad, isn't that right? Don't you—don't you want to be alive on the days that aren't so bad?"

"Every day is bad. Every day. I'm not saying it couldn't be worse. I know how some people suffer and still they cling to life. But to me this isn't life. Life is taking a walk, visiting my children, eating! Remember how I loved to eat? The *thought* of food makes me sick now." She closed her eyes. "Everything makes me sick now. This isn't life. If I had life I'd want it. I don't want this." She looked up at me the same way she had before, in the same hard-eyed way.

"Mother," I said, holding each word before letting it go, "is that really what you want—to die?"

"Of course I want to die," she said. "Next to the happiness of my children, I want to die more than anything in the world."

15

chapter

With the switch thrown, the motor in my head began to whir. Slowly at first, evenly. Then faster, louder. Who to call, I kept thinking as my feet skimmed the sidewalk home, who to call? I felt no grand emotions, only that I had a job to do now, a research assignment, a very important research assignment, and I had better do it well.

Part of doing it well, I knew, was doing it carefully. I had read all of those news stories about people who pulled plugs and the trouble they got into. Of course that's not what I was doing. I was doing research, that's all. It can't be illegal to gather information, I said to myself as I waited for the light to change on Fifth Avenue. But how to get the information? That was the problem. It's okay for me to find out how a person can die, but it's not okay for a doctor to tell me how. I knew that much.

I crossed the avenue and walked very slowly across Fifty-fifth Street toward our apartment. What doctor is going to give me suicide advice when to do so would be to risk losing his license? Or maybe even to be prosecuted? Obviously, it would have to be a friend. I had reached our building; I stood at the door for a moment before going inside. Even if I had such a friend—and offhand I couldn't think of one—it was a lot to ask.

The doctor I decided to call was someone I had known and liked since childhood. He also knew my mother and knew of her illness, although when I got him on the phone I refrained from mentioning her directly. It was neither a smooth nor a comfortable conversation. I stammered on the questions and he stiffened on the answers. I began by telling him that I planned to ask him some hypothetical questions about a good method of suicide for someone who was dying of cancer, that I wouldn't tell him why I wanted to know, and that if he wanted to discontinue the conversation at any point, he could do that. I also assured him that I was not collecting information for my own use. For a moment he said nothing. Then he cleared his throat. And finally: "All right."

I went on to explain that the person for whom I sought the information had access to the drug Dalmane. (Academic, I knew, since at the moment she couldn't keep anything down, but I assumed an eventual improvement in that.) "Would Dalmane . . . do it?" I asked. "And if so, how many . . . how many tablets of thirty milligrams would it . . . would be necessary?"

He cleared his throat before he spoke. "I can tell you," he said very slowly, "that if a person had such a wish— and I know no person who does—twenty-five is a number that . . . might prove effective."

He's scared, I thought. He's really scared. "Suppose," I said slowly, "that a person has difficulty ingesting food or anything else. Could the number twenty-five be whittled down? To ten, say?"

"I would be skeptical of that." I could hear him pulling back.

"Fifteen?"

"It's hard to say." Polite still, but clipped. No extra words, not one. That's it, I thought. That's all I'm going to get from him. "Thanks," I said. "Thanks very, very much."

There had to be a better way. I sat down on my bed and stared at the bedside lamp. After no more than five seconds I remembered Derek Humphry, a man I had interviewed once for "Nightline." He had helped his wife die and wrote a book about it called *Jean's Way*. Afterwards, he had founded some kind of pro-euthanasia group in Los Angeles called the Hemlock Society. I searched through my files, found his number, and left a message on his answering machine. Then I realized that he was probably the last person who would give me advice. As one of the heads of the movement to legalize euthanasia, he was probably watched like a convict on parole. He had published a second book, however, after the one about his wife. Now that I thought about it— I got up and went to the bookshelves in the study—yes, I had it. *Let Me Die Before I Wake*. I leafed through it, remembering now that the book contained stories about people who had killed themselves and how they did it.

Ed came home to find me sitting on the floor of the study, bent over the book. "What are you doing?"

"Reading."

"I can see that. What's so fascinating that you didn't make it into a chair?"

I looked up. He was standing right next to me, his briefcase still in his hand. "My mother wants to kill herself and

I'm trying to find out how she can do it."

Ed put his briefcase down and backed into his desk chair. I went on, "She's talked about it before and I never paid much attention. But she brought it up tonight in a way that made me think she means it."

"What way?"

Ed is a pale man, carrying still the physical legacy of a bookish adolescence—one in which indoor study is preferable to outdoor play. I love his paleness. It strikes something tender in me. But now—perhaps it was the overhead light—he looked too pale, almost ill. "I don't know," I said, on the floor still, leaning back on my wrists. "She just sounded . . . serious. She didn't really ask me to help. I don't think she wanted to ask, but she did." I straightened myself up and shook my head as if to wake myself up. "It's hard to imagine that she'd ever actually *do* such a thing. Besides, I don't see how she *could* do it. This book tells about all the different kinds of pills you can take, but she'd never be able to keep pills down." I looked up at Ed. He was staring down at the pool of light on his desk. "She's very frightened," I said. "She feels trapped in life, and I think she just wants to know there's a way out. She wants to know where the emergency door is; in fact, that's the expression she used. 'Where's the door?' she said. Even if she doesn't use it, I think she'd feel better knowing where it is." I got up, walked to the window and leaned on the sill. "Do you blame her? If you were in her shoes, wouldn't you want to know? I would. I *do*. I want to know in case it happens to me. I want to know for all of us."

"What's the book?"

I told him, and about the call to my doctor friend. He nodded slowly. I looked at him. Ed is not a quick reactor. Nor does he have the sort of face that tells emotion. I didn't know how he was taking all of this and it was starting to make me nervous.

"I agree with you." he finally said in a low voice. "I don't think she'd do anything either, but she'd certainly get some comfort knowing there was something she *could* do. So we should find out. We should find out as soon as we can."

I caught the *we*. It didn't surprise me, but it moved me. *"Don't say son-in-law . . . "* My mother is right, I thought. Ed walked over to the window where I was standing and in what felt like slow motion we wrapped our arms around each other and, for a moment, just stood there, not speaking, not moving. Then I put the pot on for tea, and we made a list of doctors we knew. Then we began to dial.

16

chapter

I had asked Belva to call me in the morning before she left and she did. "What kind of night was it, Belva?" When she paused, my heart sank.

"Not so good, Miss Rollin."

"Did she throw up again?"

"Well, yes."

"How many times?"

"Three times." I could barely hear her.

Oh God. "What about now?"

"She's resting now. Pearl's just come. Perhaps she'll have a better day today."

"Yes ... Thanks so much, Belva. Thanks for calling."

"You're most welcome, Miss Rollin."

A quarter to eight. I waited until eight, then called Dr. Goldman. "Is she keeping down any liquid at all?"

I told him no. "Her bowels aren't functioning, either."

"Hmmm. Why don't you give me a call this afternoon. If she's the same, maybe she ought to come into the hospital."

"Dr. Goldman, she may not ... what happens if she doesn't want to go the hospital?"

"Well, if she's dehydrated, I don't see any other way. She'll need an IV and we can only do that in the hospital."

"Otherwise what?"

"Otherwise she'll die."

I paused, not for long. "You know she wants to die."

"Not that way she doesn't."

And so began the fourth of October, 1983, a day we referred to later as Terrible Tuesday. I missed most of it because I spent the hours between noon and three o'clock (absurdity coming up) at the Plaza Hotel, having lunch and being honored for my reporting and writing. The other guests of honor were Roberta Peters, the opera singer, and Matilda Cuomo, wife of the governor of New York. The awards were given by a Jewish organization trying to raise money for (irony coming up) a nursing home in the Bronx.

Originally when I got the invitation I had thought it would be the sort of thing my mother would enjoy. That's an understatement; she would have adored it. When it became clear that she would not be able to go, I wanted to cancel. Shany and Ed immediately talked me out of it. First of all, said Ed, it was rude to the organization. And they both pointed out that if my mother couldn't go, she'd at least want to hear about it. But after Belva's report I was newly determined to cancel. Then I spoke to my mother. When I called her in the morning she could barely speak, but she managed to croak one question, "This is the day of the lunch, isn't it?" I admitted it was and mentioned that I might not go.

"Do you want to make me sicker?" she asked, without waiting for an answer. "If you want to make me sicker, then don't go to that lunch."

I went to the lunch. I remember two things about it, both of which stunned me even more than they shamed me: one, that I ate like a mastodon, and two, that the sight of Roberta Peters's healthy mother, who sat next to me, made me envious and sad. I also remember, at two-thirty P.M., making a Cinderella run for the pay phone in the lobby.

When I dialed my mother's number and heard Ed's voice, I thought at first that I must have dialed our number by mistake. But Ed explained in whispers what had happened, giving me the story sketchily on the phone. I learned details later. My mother's bad night had turned into a worse day. At about noon Ed got a call from Pearl saying that she couldn't keep down any of the pain medication. Ed called Dr. Goldman, who said he'd try to have her admitted to the hospital. An hour later—by this time my mother was doubled over in agony—Goldman called back with the news that there were no beds. Although he could have her admitted as an emergency, he didn't want to because if another emergency came in and took precedence, she could get "bounced" to another hospital. When Ed told him about the pain getting worse—by now Ed was at the apartment with her—Dr. Goldman suggested calling a private nursing service. They would send over a nurse, he said, who would give her a shot (which Pearl, as an aide, wasn't licensed to do). Meanwhile Dr. Goldman would write out a prescription for the shot medication and for the syringes the nurse would need to give it to her.

Ed left my mother with Pearl and Shany, who had arrived by then, ran uptown to Dr. Goldman's office, picked up the prescription, got it filled, and ran back to the apartment where a nurse was waiting. The nurse tore open Ed's package and, as quickly as she could (by now my mother was begging for relief), plunged a needle filled with two cc's of Demerol into my mother's right hip. She fell asleep almost immediately, Ed said, and was still sleeping now. He had hired the nurse for a full shift in case my mother needed another shot. Shany planned to stay around too, so why didn't I just go home. "It's getting pretty crowded around here," he said. "I'm leaving soon myself."

As we hung up I felt my lunch double back into my throat. I lurched toward the ladies' room and made it in time. Afterwards, on my way out through the carpeted lobby, I thought of my poor mother's dry retching and how easy it was, by contrast, to throw up three lovely courses from the Plaza Hotel.

As soon as I got home, I took off my dress and got into bed. I heard the front door open and close. "Ed?"

"Yep."

"I'm in bed."

"That's a good idea. How was lunch?"

"Don't ask. How are *you?*"

"Fine." He took off his jacket and sat down on the edge of the bed. I sat up and leaned against the headboard.

"You look beat," I said. "I'm sorry you had to . . . I'm sorry about today."

"It wasn't your fault. You don't look so hot yourself."

"I'm okay. What's happening over there now?"

"No change. She's out cold. The nurse stayed. Another one will come at ten and be there until ten tomorrow morning."

"Did you—"

"I called Belva. I told her we'd pay her anyway, but not to come."

"What happens tomorrow?"

"Tomorrow the other nurse comes back. I canceled Pearl and told her the same thing. Of course tomorrow, with a little luck, she'll get into the hospital." He pulled off his shoes, leaned his elbows on his knees, and made a slow circle with his head. I got out from under the covers, crawled down the length of the bed, and held him around the waist, the side of my face on his back. "How did I get so lucky? Who has such a husband?"

"Cut it out," he said with a laugh. "You sound like your mother."

"What's wrong with that?" I said, holding him tighter. "She had your number from the start. By the way," I said, letting go a little, "she's not going to want to go to the hospital. Once she's in the hospital she won't be able to . . . do anything."

"She won't be able to 'do anything' anywhere at this point. She can't swallow one pill. You should have seen her trying to keep down one Dalmane. She kept talking to herself, as if she could talk it down. 'Maybe if I sit up; maybe if I stand up; maybe if I crush it in some tea . . .' Then the pain got so bad she couldn't even *talk* about swallowing."

"I know," I interrupted, falling back on the bed, not wanting to hear more. "Pills won't work. We'll have to think of something else."

"Did you speak to Fred?" Fred was another doctor we knew, an acquaintance and hardly even that. At this point we were calling anyone we could think of with an M.D. who was not a member of Right To Life.

"Yes. He said that fifteen Dalmane would probably do it if she could get them down, but it sounded to him as if she couldn't."

"Fifteen? What's-his-name said twenty-five! How are we supposed to know which is right? Maybe neither is right! How the hell are we supposed to *know?*" I got out of bed and pulled on a bathrobe and sat back down next to Ed on the bed. My stomach felt odd, as if it had been hollowed out. "What about cars? Don't people do it in cars? Isn't that painless? How does that work, anyway? Do you know?"

"It's carbon monoxide," he said slowly. "You attach a tube from the exhaust pipe into the car and shut the doors and windows. Or you can do it in a garage. Close the garage door and start the car. The other way's probably quicker, though."

"We don't have a car."

"I realize that."

I stood up, shoved my hands in my bathrobe pockets, and began walking around the room as if it were a track.

"Maybe we could rent one." Ed shook his head. "Or borrow one," I went on, "from a friend. I'm serious. Think how simple it would be. All she has to do is sit there."

"And where do you do this?" said Ed, less quietly than before. "On Fifth Avenue? Second Avenue? Or do we drive her to Brooklyn in the middle of the night? And what do we tell the police?"

I leaned against the wall and looked at my husband, who was still sitting on the foot of the bed as if it were a park bench. He hadn't even loosened his tie. "What's the matter with us?" I said. "Don't stupid people figure out how to make people die every day? Why can't we? If they can, why can't we?" I glared at Ed and Ed glared at the carpet. The sound of a bird came from the courtyard. I turned toward the window. There it was again. Cheep. Then again, cheep. The bird sounded sick. I shut the window. "What about a gun?" I said.

"We don't have a gun."

"We could buy one."

"That's asking for trouble. There are records kept of people who buy guns. Also, I don't think your mother would go for that."

"Do we know anyone who has a gun?"

Ed shook his head. "I don't, do you?"

"I guess not. Not *my* liberal friends. Democrats in favor of gun control don't own guns. I wish we lived in Texas. Even Democrats have guns in Texas."

"We could get in touch with that Puerto Rican gang you did a story on for NBC. Remember?"

"Are you kidding?"

"Yes."

"Well, maybe we should. It's going to take something crazy, you know. That's what it's going to take."

"What're you going to do? Hire a bunch of thugs to shoot your mother?"

"Not at all. I'd just ask them if she could borrow their gun. They'd do it. They liked me. I put them on television."

"You're not serious. Tell me you're not serious."

"I'm ... groping."

"I'll say."

"I still think a gun is something to think about. It's quick and it's deadly. Isn't that why we're against them?"

"And who's going to pull the trigger? You?"

"My mother could do it herself, couldn't she? Is it hard to pull a trigger? I never have. Have you?"

"Yes."

"Is it hard?"

"Not really. It ... it can be adjusted."

"So?"

"So what? You still have to have a gun in order to shoot

it, and we don't have a gun and we can't get a gun. Anyway, who are we fooling? Can you imagine your mother pulling a trigger?"

I sighed and slowly slid down the wall until my seat hit the floor. I looked up. "Well, Professor, what's your idea?"

"I've been thinking about arsenic. But from what I understand it's ... messy. Besides—same problem as a gun—I don't know where we'd get it."

"What do you mean, messy?"

"I think it produces convulsions. Cyanide is probably better. That's what Goering used—Hitler too, I think—but again, where in hell do you get cyanide?"

"There's good old-fashioned wrist-slashing, but if she wanted to do that she would have said so by now." I shuddered. "No, it can't be anything that ugly ... or violent. My mother would never do anything violent." I stood up and walked the length of the room and back again.

"I know what our problem is. Our problem is that we're amateurs. What do we know about what makes people die? Nothing. But our further problem is that the people who *do* know, the professionals, are criminals. And I agree with you, we can't talk to them. The other professionals are doctors, who won't talk to *us*. So what do we do? What the *hell* do we do? I mean, the more I think about it, the more I can understand her wanting out. Look at today. And what's tomorrow going to be? And I don't even want to think about next week or, God, next month. I mean this can—will—go *on*. If there's no treatment that thing inside her will get bigger, and the bigger it gets the more it'll hurt. Won't it? Isn't that right? Isn't that *logical*?"

"I'm going to make some calls tomorrow about other

chemicals," said Ed, half to himself. "Maybe there's something else I don't know about that's easier to get."

"You know something?" I said, staring at the windowpane. "With all our big talk, none of this is real to me. When I really think about it. I can't . . . I can't imagine her actually doing it. Can you? Can you?"

"Yes. But in a way that's not the issue. The issue is choice. She says she wants to die, and at the very least she means she wants to be able to die. She wants to have the choice and I think we should see to it that she gets it."

For a moment we were both silent. Then I sighed a huge, heaved sigh and looked at my husband.

"But you do think she'd do it? Tell me why you think that. Tell me why?"

"Because it makes sense, and your mother's sensible. And because what happened to my mother didn't make sense. And she knows that. I'm sure she thinks about my mother."

"I'm sure she does, too," I said. We were side by side at the foot of the bed now, our eyes fixed on the turned-off TV on the opposite wall. "I think about her—what happened to her—all the time, don't you?"

Ed nodded. "I think about those last days. I think about sitting at her bedside and how I wanted to put a pillow over her face."

"Why didn't you?"

He looked at me. "Because . . . because you don't kill your mother."

"What's the difference between that and what we're doing? I know, but I want you to tell me."

He looked at me again. "There's every difference. We're not talking about killing your mother. We're talking about her killing herself. The other difference is that your mother *wants* to kill herself. My mother wanted God to do it." Ed stood up suddenly and walked toward the door. Without turning around he added, "She couldn't imagine that God would let her down." He was out the door now, on his way into the study. "I'm going to do mathematics for a little while."

"Okay," I said, half wishing as I sometimes did that I could do mathematics too.

17

chapter

The chart had a third handwriting now, the smooth script of the new nurse, a thin, neat, uniformed white woman in her fifties with clear blue eyes, a long, bony nose, and a slight accent I couldn't place.

3:45 P.M. Demerol, 1 cc	Patient resting comfortably
6:45 P.M. Demerol, 1 cc	until 6 P.M. Sponge bath.
	Takes few sips of water. Pain
Voided.	medicated. Daughter and son-
	in-law arrive at 9 P.M.

"I've never had shots like that," said my mother. "She has the hands of an angel. Did you ever hear of a six-inch needle going in and you feel nothing? Did you ever hear of such a thing?"

"Now Mrs. Rollin," said the nurse, fighting off a blush, "your daughter and son-in-law didn't come to hear about your injections."

As soon as the nurse left the room, my mother wiggled her finger for us to come closer. "I don't know about this one," she whispered. "She left her husband and two children in Czechoslovakia. A ten-year-old and a twelve-year-old. Left them, just like that. You have to be a tough cookie to do that."

She wanted to hear about the lunch, mainly about who said what wonderful thing about me and what wonderful thing I said back. And what did I wear? And what did Matilda Cuomo and Roberta Peters wear? I told her what she wanted to know, omitting the closing moments in the ladies' room and omitting any mention of Roberta Peters's mother.

"And how is my handsome son-in-law? I should say son. Who else would have—"

"Fine, Ida. It sure is good to see you looking so much better. Quite a difference from this afternoon."

"Don't remind me. It's all in that needle. I'll probably become a dope addict now." She smiled. "I guess they won't arrest me, not that I'd mind if they gave me the electric chair. But they won't give you the electric chair unless you don't want it. It's a crazy world."

She let her head drop back on the pillow, then lifted it and signaled us to come closer. "So what have you found out?"

"About what?" I said, wanting to be sure. I had a self-made rule never to bring the subject up until my mother brought it up first.

"You know," she said. And whenever she did bring it up—although it rarely surprised me, although I wanted for her what she wanted for herself, although I was proud of her for wanting it—whenever she did bring it up, I felt my heart crack a little.

"I . . . we . . . found out a few things."

The subject hadn't come up before in front of Ed. She didn't seem to notice. She assumed he knew. The closeness behind her assumption moved me, but I tried not to be moved. I didn't want to be moved anymore. I didn't want to feel anything anymore. It was too dangerous now to feel things. I was a soldier with a battle ahead. Feelings could muck everything up.

"What did you find out?" she asked.

I turned around to make sure the nurse was out of earshot.

"Maybe these," I said, picking up the Dalmane.

"How many?"

"Probably around fifteen . . . or more."

"Who told you?"

"Fred Silver."

"You called him?" I nodded. "Isn't that sweet," said my mother. "I always thought he was a nice boy." She looked at the bottle again and frowned. "How will I be able to take fifteen pills?"

"That's the problem," I said. "But we're gathering other ideas."

"What other ideas?"

Oh God, I thought, please stop.

She sighed and turned her head toward the wall. "Maybe you could take me to the roof of this building. I hear it's nice up there."

I looked down at my hands. It was getting hard to tell when something was a joke. "Your digestion could improve, Mother. That could happen."

She nodded. "So I can't die until I feel better."

"It looks that way now, Ida," said Ed softly, "but leave it to us. We're just starting to find out . . . what we need to know. Please don't worry about it."

My mother sighed. Then she looked at us with her big eyes and with no warning turned into a sad six-year-old. "Why do I have to go to the hospital tomorrow? I'll never be able to do it in the hospital."

"I know that, Mother. . ." I leaned over and straightened out her little white cap, which had slipped back on her head. Her scalp with its few wispy hairs had become as private a place on her body as her genitals. "But in the hospital they can probably get your body functioning again."

"They'll start doing other things too," she frowned. "They're not going to let me alone."

She was right. When she got to the hospital the next day we found out that Dr. Goldman had ordered a blood transfusion. I called him from her bedside phone. "She doesn't want it," I told him.

"She'll feel better if she has it. She's anemic."

"I know, but she's tired of being propped up." I looked down at my mother and she pumped her head up and down. "She wants to be . . . let go," I said, turning back to the telephone.

"I hear you, but blood transfusion or no blood transfusion, Betty, your mother is going to hang on for a while whether she wants to or not, and the transfusion will just give her a little more energy."

"Okay," I said, "I'll tell her that," and I did, but she shook her head.

"I don't want it," she said. "I don't want it."

She got better, even without the transfusion. The pain subsided—she went off Demerol after one night—and the

IV reversed her dehydration. But as her body perked up, her spirits took off in another direction. It wasn't depression this time, but anger.

She snapped at the nurse's aide who took her blood pressure, she barked at Shany, she even let me have it. When I came by later in the day with some talcum powder she'd asked for, she took it out of the bag and threw it down on the bed. "It's too small," she mumbled. "I told you to get a bigger one. I'll use this up in one day."

Not like her, not like her at all. And when they wheeled in another patient—a lovely, refined sort of woman in her sixties who, we found out, also had cancer—my mother not only failed to gather pertinent details of the woman's life, she barely said hello to her.

"You seem angry," I said to her finally. She looked startled. I thought she'd deny it. Instead she said, "I am."

"Who at?" She gave me the same look. "Me?"

"That's a stupid question," she said. "Why should I be angry at you? I'm angry because I'm stuck."

"What do you mean, stuck?"

"I'm stuck—stuck in life. I don't want to be here anymore. I don't see why I can't get out. And I'm so tired of them telling me how great I look and how well I'm doing. Sometimes I feel like turning around and looking behind me to see who they're talking to. I feel lousy. I feel lousy all the time. Sometimes it's more, sometimes it's less. These doctors don't understand what it *feels* like to be sick this way. All they know is your blood pressure and your temperature and the size of your tumor. They don't *hear* you when you tell them how you feel. And they definitely don't hear you when you tell them you want to take a powder."

"I guess they don't know how to deal with that." As I spoke, my mind shot along another track. She means it. I think she really means it. Is it possible? Is it possible she will actually do this thing?

"These doctors," she shook her head. "This partner of Dr. Goldman's came by this morning. I forget his name, I can't remember anything any more. So he came and he sat down right here on the chair next to my bed. I must say, that was nice of him. None of the other doctors sit down. If a person sits down, it's like you're having a conversation. When they stand over you, they're way up there, and you always feel they can't wait to go. Remember how Dr. Burns used to do that? When they stand like that I can never remember what I want to ask them, not that it matters. I'm sick of the questions. I'm sick of the answers. What was I talking about anyway? I forgot what I was saying. You see? Now my mind is going."

"There's nothing wrong with your mind, Mother. You were talking about why you felt so angry."

"Oh, that's right. Well, it was this partner of Dr. Goldman's whose name I can't remember. So he sat down and he started this how-are-you business and I said, how do you think I am? Why can't you just give me a pill so I can get out of this? Why can't you do that? Look, I told him, they kill murderers! Didn't that Norman what's-his-name write a book about a murderer who wanted to go to the electric chair and they said okay, fine. So if they say okay, fine to him, why can't they say it to me?"

"Mother, what are they supposed to do? Take you to prison and put you in an electric chair?"

"No, I'll make it easy for them. No prison, no electric chairs. They can do it right here. They can just give me a shot right here. This doctor—the nice one who sits down—he says to me, 'Mrs. Rollin, you're an intelligent woman. You're full of vitality. What do you want to die for?' Have you ever heard anything so stupid? Vitality!

To him this is vitality! I'm half dead. My only problem is the other half. Now here comes another one."

I turned around to see a resident, who looked sicker than my mother. He had a syringe in his hand. "You see?" she said. "They don't leave me alone."

The resident smiled vacantly and made his way toward my mother's vein. "Make a fist please."

"Blood again," said my mother. "They're always taking blood. I'm surprised I have any left." She looked at the resident who was lost in his search for a vein. "Why can't you put a little poison in there?"

"Mother, cut it out. This man is a resident. He's doing his job. He's probably been up for forty-seven hours."

"I'm sorry," said my mother, giving him one of her I'm-only-a-little-girl-I-can't-help-it looks. "Ouch. You see? They hurt you, but they won't kill you."

She wouldn't let up. Late the next afternoon her bedside telephone went out of order. A repairman came to fix it, took it apart, and then—reason unknown—walked out without putting it back together. A nurse with the face of a cherub and the body of a fullback happened to walk in a few minutes later. "Wha's this?" she bellowed (the voice went with the body, not with the face) when she saw the phone. When I explained, she bent over it as if it were a coiled rattler. "I ain't touchin' this thing!" she said. "A person who touches this thing could get 'lectrocuted." My mother, who had her eyes closed, opened them and in her small, hoarse voice cried out, "I'll touch it! Move it over here, I'll touch it!" But the nurse didn't hear. She was already on her way out of the room, missing my mother's little joke. Her little half-joke.

That night a novelist friend stepped into the breach. He called an internist he knew and said he was writing a short story in which the main character wants to kill himself. However, our friend explained to the internist, the character's digestion is screwed up and he can't swallow pills; nor has he access to a gun or an automobile. What then, for the story, would such a person do?

The internist—tickled, apparently, at the prospect of lending a literary hand—immediately proffered two solutions; one, dehydration, and two, the injection of air into a vein.

Dr. Goldman had given me the distinct impression that death by dehydration was too ghastly to consider, but I thought I'd check it out one more time. Now using fiction as my own ruse, I called yet another physician, a friend of a friend this time. He promptly confirmed what Dr. Goldman had implied, that dehydration wouldn't do. Even if the process began naturally—that is, even if her digestive system stopped functioning again and she began to dehydrate on her own—not treating it would make her "extremely uncomfortable." It occurred to me that my mother might have been brave enough to face the discomfort, but I decided I was not brave enough to watch it. Nor could I bear what the doctor said would happen next. She would slip into a coma and her bodily functions would go out of control. How on earth would we deal with that? Worst of all was the duration. As I understood it, she wouldn't necessarily die right away. It could be days, even weeks. The more we heard, the more sickening it sounded.

An air bubble seemed like a better idea by far. But who would give it to her? "Easy," I said to Ed. "All we have to do is find someone who doesn't mind being indicted for murder."

"Maybe she can do it herself," Ed said. "We have syringes."

"She doesn't know how."

"She could learn."

"Who's going to teach her?"

"A nurse could teach her. Don't we have any friends who are nurses?"

In fact, we did. Not a friend, exactly, but a friend's sister who had been a nurse. My friend called her sister and reported back to us that the sister felt sympathetic and might have helped us, but when her husband, a psychoanalyst, got wind of it, he said absolutely she would do no such thing. My friend mentioned that he did ask whether my mother was depressed. If so, he offered to recommend medication for depression.*

I saw no point in giving my mother chapter and verse on all of this. I didn't want her lying in bed with specific, clear pictures in her mind of how she night do herself in. Usually she didn't press for details; a general update seemed to suffice. "How's it going?" she'd say, or "Anything new?" as if she were asking about my latest television assignment.

"It's going okay," I'd say. I didn't want her lying in bed thinking we weren't getting anywhere either, even though we weren't.

We had one of those what's-new exchanges when I visited her in the hospital the following day. And she sounded one new note. "I hope what you're doing won't get you into trouble," she said, eyeing me. "If it will, I want you to stop."

"It's not a crime to do research." I told her.

She looked skeptical. "Are you sure?"

"I'm sure." And I was. But if we succeeded in finding a

*Later I learned that the air bubble method is, in fact, both painful and ineffective.

way, and if the way worked—if it actually happened—then, I thought, we'll be in trouble. Maybe.

Either way I couldn't worry about it now. Ed seemed of the same mind. "We'll help her as much as we can," he said, "and when it's over, if we have a problem, we have a problem."

We also thought, we should be so lucky.

18
chapter

October 6. When I arrived at the hospital the next morning I did a double take. The IV had been disconnected and my mother was holding up to her face something that looked like a sandwich. If I had to guess, I would have said a chicken sandwich. By now I should have been used to reversals. Cancer was wacky. Tumors press harder some days than others. I knew all about it. But a chicken sandwich? My God, she had it in her mouth.

The curtains between my mother's bed and her roommate's had been pulled open—the roommate was also having lunch—and the two of them were going at it like a couple of ladies in the Palm Court of the Plaza Hotel. As I entered, my mother was saying, mouth full (mouth full!), "Your son sounds like my son-in-law. I should say my son because . . ."

While I gaped, my mother introduced me to the other woman, the one she had cut dead the day before. I nodded hello and kissed my mother and, as long as they were in the middle of a conversation, excused myself and stepped out into the corridor. I wanted a little space to absorb what I had just seen. I wanted to think. But I didn't know what to think. She was eating. If she could eat food she could swallow pills. But if she's eating, I thought, and if she looks as cheerful as she looks right now in that room chitchatting with that woman, does she *want* to swallow pills? She can't want to. She can't. Slowly I began to walk down the hallway. My feet hardly moved, but my head was racing.

This whole suicide business never seemed like anything that would actually happen, anyhow. So theatrical, suicide, so out of proportion. It was almost a matter of scale. Suicide had such girth; my mother was so very little. By the time I had walked the length of the hospital corridor, everything seemed clear. We could still continue to gather information. It still made sense to try to find out "where the door is," as she put it, so that she wouldn't feel trapped. But suddenly it seemed absurd to think she would ever push the door open and go through it.

When I walked back into the room, the sight of her confirmed what I had been thinking. She looked almost healthy. She looked happy. She looked like my mother. She did not look like someone who would make herself die. We'll handle this, I thought. I'll call Hospice again. We'll deal with what comes. I sat down on the chair next to her bed. I felt better than I had felt in weeks. I felt as if a large, ticking package had just been removed from my arms.

The roommate had begun a slow shuffle from her bed toward the door. "Look how you're walking, Phyllis," my mother said, smiling encouragement. "*Much* better than yesterday."

As soon as she went out the door, my mother's expression changed. "I can eat," she said, holding up the half-empty sandwich plate as if it were Exhibit A. "I can digest food. I tried the sandwich on purpose. It's staying down. I'd know by now if it wasn't."

I said nothing. My mother was looking at me, the sandwich plate still in her hand. "Do you know what I'm telling you? I can eat. I'm unblocked, Dr. Goldman says. Before, I was blocked. Now I'm unblocked. I can eat food. If I can eat food, I can eat pills."

Slowly I nodded. My head felt heavy. "Mother, do you mean . . . do you still want to . . . ?"

She looked annoyed. "Of course I want to."

"But you seem so well," I said. I felt like crying. I didn't, but she must have noticed because her tone of voice changed.

"Sweetheart, I'm having a good day. That doesn't mean anything. The tumor's still there. It's giving me a little vacation. So that's nice. I hope to God it lasts a few days, but nothing's changed."

"How do you know nothing's changed?"

"I asked Dr. Goldman."

"When? What did he say?"

"Early this morning, after breakfast. I ate breakfast too, you know; cereal I ate, almost half a bowl and a little juice and coffee. That's more than I've eaten in two weeks. So I asked him what it meant, because to feel almost like a human being after you haven't felt like a human being in such a long time is—"

"What did he say?"

"Well, he hemmed and he hawed, he said this and that,

but what it boiled down to was that I could have a day like this or a few days, he didn't know, but the tumor was there, big as ever and growing. They took X rays yesterday; it was so cold down there I thought I'd die. There I go, wishful thinking again. Anyway, it's there and it's just a matter of time before it starts pushing again at my bowel and intestines, blocking me up and making me miserable again. I wasn't surprised by what he said. Your mother has never believed in miracles. But it made me think I better get out of this hospital quick, because I won't be able to do anything while I'm here, right?"

"No, I mean yes, that's right . . . So you want us to find out about pills again?"

"Sure! But first I've got to get out of here. Dr. Goldman said tomorrow, maybe."

"You asked him that, too?"

"Sure. He didn't think anything about it. He knows I hate the hospital."

That evening we hit the research again in earnest. I began by going back to the Humphry book, which didn't quite tell us what we needed to know. From it I learned that fifteen Dalmane (she still had that many since she now got shots for pain) would not have been effective. Humphry quotes another book as recommending no fewer than twenty tablets of thirty-milligram Dalmane, adding that the tablets should be only "used in conjunction with other methods." But the book fails to say what the other methods are.*

I kept turning pages and twice reread a story about a woman who committed suicide by taking one and a half grams, described as "the minimum lethal dose," of Seconal.

* Unknown to us at the time, later editions of the Humphry book, published by Hemlock Society/Grove Press, contained more explicit instructions. Some years later, Humphry's book, *Final Exit*, for which I wrote an introduction, revealed still more.

But the woman was very "tiny" and "frail." My mother was not; her face was gaunt, but her body, even with a loss of twenty-five pounds, retained its fleshiness.

In a way, the parts of the book that helped us most—and at the same time alarmed us—were the parts about aiming for death and missing. The frail woman who succeeded with Seconal first attempted to kill herself by taking an insufficient dose of Dalmane and whiskey and wound up in a hospital having her stomach pumped. I read the story aloud to Ed and we promptly and solemnly vowed that if we—she—did this thing, she had better do it right.

Meanwhile I went back to pushing buttons on the telephone. Even if we were able to piece together a plan from the Humphry book, it seemed risky to proceed without some direct guidance from a doctor. By now we had reached the bottom of our list of doctors in New York and had moved on to the West Coast. I had a surge of hope when a Los Angeles internist I knew answered the phone. I guessed he would approve of what we were trying to do in principle—and I think he did—but when it came to practice he wasn't about to stick his neck out. He pretended to, though. "You could try a grain and a half of a barbiturate," he said, speaking so fast I couldn't quite get it.

"A grain?" I shouted. "Harry, did you say a grain or a gram?"

"Yeah," he said. "Yeah, that's right. Look, I wish I could be more help, but I see I've got a patient . . ."

"Oh sure, Harry. That's okay. You helped a lot. Thanks very much."

"Don't mention it." Click.

"I don't blame them," I said to Ed. "I really don't. It's against the law to give this kind of advice and they're scared. I could choke Harry, but I can't blame him."

So for the moment we gave up on doctors. I placed the

next call to a friend who's father is a pharmacist. She knew all about my mother's illness and said she'd do anything to help. Of course she'd call her father and ask him whatever we wanted to know. "Make sure," I said to her, "that your father understands we are not asking him to supply us with drugs. We only want information. We want to know what would work. Once we know that, we can take it from there."

Our friend was so anxious to help she couldn't wait to get off the phone with me and get after her father. "I'll call you in five minutes!" she said. An hour later she reported back to us that, after a lengthy argument, her father had told her that under no circumstances would he give out such information. He was upset with her for asking and suggested that my mother ask her doctor for medication for pain and nausea.

"I'm so sorry," my friend said, obviously distressed. "I wouldn't have believed my father would react that way. At first I thought he didn't understand. But he didn't seem to *want* to understand. I kept explaining it over and over and finally when I cornered him, he blew up. I can't get over how—"

"Don't worry about it," I said, and made a thumbs-down signal to Ed. "Thanks a lot for trying. We really appreciate it."

I hung up and fell into a chair. Ed fell into a chair on the other side of a room and we stared at each other. "Now what?" I asked.

"I don't know," Ed said. "I took another look at the Humphry book. It *is* possible to figure out from what's in here what she'd need to take, but all of the drugs mentioned require a heavy dose—many, many pills. Most of the dosages listed are in grams, but most drugs come in milligrams, so in some cases she'd need to take forty, fifty pills. Even though her digestions good now, I doubt if it's *that* good. And of course that's only part of the problem. The other part is that we don't *have* the stuff and I can't imagine how we're going to get it."

"Maybe we're going about this wrong. Maybe we should forget doctors and try to think of people who take drugs who might have a surplus."

"Who do we know who takes drugs?"

"No one, damn it. I can't even think of anyone we know who takes Valium! Wait a minute." I sat straight up. "I just thought of someone. Maryanne."

"Maryanne? Maryanne's not exactly a junkie."

"No, but remember she's had cancer—uterine, I think—and she's been taking drugs for pain. I know she has because she told me."

"Call her."

"I will, but I'm trying to think how to do it without upsetting her. She's nowhere near as sick as my mother, but she's been pretty sick and I don't want to give her any ideas."

"I wouldn't worry. I'm sure Maryanne is struggling to live at this point, not die."

So I called my friend Maryanne. She was wonderful. She was even exuberant. She made such a dash for her medicine cabinet that she dropped the telephone on the floor. "Are you there? Are you there? Oh, I'm sorry, wait a minute, okay? Don't go away, okay? I won't be long; I *know* I've got something. Oh you poor dears, but you're doing the right thing. Listen, I've thought of it myself—down the line, I mean. Wait a minute now, I'll be right back. Okay, let's see, I just grabbed everything I have and I'll read you the labels, okay? Okay, here's one. Percodan. Percodan. Okay? And here's another one. Dil-au-did. Di-laudid. Got that? Okay, here's another. Lev-o- . . ." And so she went, ticking them off one by one, and reading me what the dosages were; then she dumped the contents of each bottle out on a table, and counted the exact number of tablets she had of each drug. "You can have all of these!" she said. "I can easily get new prescriptions from my doctor. Do you want me to bring them up to you? I can do that *easily!* It's no trouble, *really!*"

Funny who comes through and who doesn't. Maryanne wasn't even a first-string friend. We had been close long ago when we were both single. After I married Ed, I tried to continue the friendship and succeeded only in part. In the last couple of years I hadn't seen much of her at all. I called her when I heard she was sick, but she had sounded so chipper, I never did anything more than call her again. Maryanne was not someone who did well in the role of Sick Person. As long as I'd known her I'd never seen her on anyone's receiving end. Sweet, quirky woman that she was, in her long ethnic dresses, surrounded always by her collection of stray animals—and stray people—her stock-in-trade was ministering to other people's needs, not having them herself.

"Maryanne," I said, hoarse from gratitude, "this is so kind of you. I don't think it makes sense to collect the pills from you now, but I've written down the drugs you have and when I find out what we need, I'll call you back. That you'd give them to us is so extraordinary, Maryanne. It's more than a help. It's . . . it's . . ."

"Don't be silly! I'm telling you, I've thought of it myself, okay? I mean, I'm fine now, I'm great, but what if things got really terrible—*terminally* terrible? I'd want to—well, at least I'd want to know how to bug out, okay? By the way, if you need someone to talk to about this, I know a terrific doctor."

"You do?"

"Yes, he's wonderful. He's an old friend and he believes in what you want to do. I know he's helped other people. You should call him."

"Oh, I will! Oh, Maryanne, we've been *searching* for a doctor who would help us. I can't tell you how ... Maryanne, is this someone we can absolutely trust?"

"What do you mean?"

"I mean does he know what he's talking about? Can we be certain if he tells us what to do that he's telling us right?"

"Yes. Absolutely yes. He's sixty-seven years old, okay? He's the straightest, smartest, nicest, most trustworthy man in the whole world. Believe me. And before he went abroad he was head of internal medicine in some big hospital in Chicago—"

"Maryanne, did you say 'abroad'?"

"He lives in Amsterdam."

"Amsterdam? You mean Holland?"

"He's American—from Louisville, as a matter of fact—but he's lived over there for a few years."

"Oh God, wouldn't you know."

"What's the difference? You can still call him, okay?"

"In Holland?"

"Why not? I'll give you his number."

Why not indeed.

From the telephone book we found out how to dial Amsterdam directly, and from the overseas operator we found out that Amsterdam was seven hours ahead of us, too late, therefore, to call right then. We set an alarm for three A.M. and woke up before the alarm went off. I sat up, shivered, and pulled the phone into bed. Ed closed the window, put on his bathrobe, and sat down in the armchair next to our bed. The silence was eerie. For a couple of seconds I stayed still and listened to it. Then, carefully, I began pushing buttons on the telephone.

I did what I always do when I'm nervous; I talked too much. I told him everything from what my mother ate that day to what drugs were in Maryanne's medicine cabinet. When I began to slow down and ask questions, the doctor began to ask questions of his own. He spoke slowly, pronouncing each syllable, as if the telephone connection weren't as good as, in fact, it was. His voice was gentle, with somewhat of a drawl. He sounded kind and also cautious. I liked that. "How long has your mother been ill? Is she depressed? Has she been depressed before? What is your state of mind right now? What about your husband? Does your mother live alone?" He asked psychological questions, medical questions, practical questions. It felt more like an interview than a conversation, and at the end I wasn't sure I had passed.

"I'd like to think about this and check on a few things and call you back," he said. "It must be very late there now. Why don't you get some sleep, and by the time you wake up I'll call you. That'll be in about five hours. Will that be all right?"

Of course, I said, and thanked him and told him to please call collect. I hung up the phone. "I think we're onto something now. He sounded good to me. He sounded . . . solid."

"Great," said Ed. "We'll know more when he calls back. Let's go to sleep."

But I couldn't sleep. I was too excited, too hopeful. I imagined him calling back to say that ten tablets of Maryanne's Percodan would do just fine. That was my favorite scenario. Then my imaginings took a turn and I all but heard his voice telling me that drugs wouldn't work and that I'd have to get a gun. Then I imagined him not calling back at all. Then I fell asleep. Then the phone rang. It was he.

The connection wasn't as good this time; I had to strain to hear. But he spoke as slowly and distinctly as he had before and I wrote down what he said. "Dalmane is not the best sort of thing to use in these circumstances," he began. "Nor are the drugs you mentioned of Maryanne's." Soundlessly, my heart sank. "If it's possible, get Nembutal. The absorption of that drug is quite fast. Then what you might do is combine the Nembutal with four or five of the Dalmane your mother already has."

"How much Nembutal?"

"I'd say twenty capsules, one hundred milligrams each, would be more than enough. With twenty you could feel quite confident you'd have the result you want."

"Doctor, do you have any idea how we might get Nembutal?"

"No, but it shouldn't be too difficult. That's partly why I thought of it. You'll need a prescription of course, but I should think your mother's internist would give it to you. Nembutal is strong, but it's quite commonly used as a medication for anxiety and sleeplessness, so your mother could say she'd like to have it."

"She has sleep medication already—the Dalmane—but I guess she could say it isn't strong enough."

"Exactly."

My heart fell further. I couldn't imagine Dr. Goldman buying that. And twenty pills. I had hoped for ten or fifteen. "Is there . . . any special way the pills should be taken?"

"Yes, I was just getting to that. What she should do first of all is refrain from having anything to eat or drink during the previous six hours, but before that—before the six hours—she should have something light to eat, like toast and tea. Then, does she have any antinausea medication?"

"She has Reglan and Compazine."

"Good. Compazine is good. Fifteen minutes before she takes the Nembutal, let her take a Compazine. That will help her keep the Nembutal down. But, as I say, it's so fast-acting I don't think you'll have a problem. These are just safety precautions. Also, I would suggest she take the Nembutal with a small amount of soda—club soda or whatever—and, let me see, oh yes, I am assuming she will be doing this at home, not in the hospital."

"Yes," I said. "We'll be taking her home in a day or two, I'm sure."

He went on. "If there is a problem at any point, do not hesitate to call me at any hour. I've told my wife about this, so that if a call comes in the middle of the night, she won't think something terrible has happened to the children."

He laughed a little and I tried to laugh with him. "How can I . . . I'm so grateful," I stammered. "I don't know if I mentioned what a hard time we had getting someone to talk to us about this . . ."

"I know," he said. "It's a problem a lot of people have. I get quite a few calls from the States."

"You do?"

"Yes. Modern medicine has done a great job of prolonging life, but the legal system hasn't caught up with the difficulties that inevitably arise when you have people living longer than they want to live." He paused as if he expected me to interrupt him. When I didn't he went on. "People should have the right to end their lives when they want to, and if they need help to do it, so be it. Well, don't get me started." He laughed his short laugh.

"Oh, please go on. I'm interested."

"Well, the other point is that one has to be very, very careful in many ways with something like this. Should suicidal assistance become legal, it must be ascertained that the person truly wants it. This can be done, of course, with an interdisciplinary board of examiners. I must tell you that most people, no matter how sick they get, don't want to die. They want to live—or they're afraid to die—and of course that's their right and everything should be done that can be done to see that they live as long as they want to live.

"Then again—I apologize, this *is* turning into a lecture!—some people *say* they want to die, but they don't. So it's very important to give people the information and the support they need, but when the moment comes, again, they must continue to have the option to do whatever it is they want to do, to take this action or not to take it. Don't be surprised if your mother changes her mind. It's entirely possible—even likely, I would say—that she will."

"I . . . I'm glad you told me all of this. It'll make me pay closer attention. It's odd. Rationally, in my mind, especially when I think of her suffering, I hope she does it. But when I hear you say she may not, I feel relieved. It's a seesaw and I've been on it from the beginning."

"And you'll probably stay on it. That's normal. You love your mother; you don't want her to die. But because you love your mother, you *do* want her to die. Whatever happens, it's not going to be easy. As I say, you should be able to work this out successfully. But call any time if you have a question. And good luck."

We ate breakfast in a hurry and took a cab up to the hospital. I felt strange. I felt the kind of excitement that usually borders happiness. But this excitement bordered nothing. Voltage without joy—it was peculiar.

I was nervous too. What if her digestion went on the blink again? What if she couldn't keep anything down? What if during the night some kind of electrical storm in her body caused a power failure? What if . . . but as soon as we walked into the room I saw on her face that the switch was on and the current was still flowing. She had the telephone cradled in her shoulder. "My gorgeous children just walked in. Yes. Okay, I'll tell them. I'll talk to you tomorrow." She handed me the receiver and I hung it up. "Alvin sends his love," she said, as we bent down to kiss her. Alvin, I thought, poor Alvin. She still won't see him, so he calls. He'll call, probably, until the end.

She looked even better than she had the day before. Her cheeks were pink; her eyes shone the way they used to. "They're sending me home tomorrow," she said. "I can hardly wait!"

Then, in her conspirator's whisper, she summoned us closer. "Tell me what's going on before she gets back." My mother gestured toward her roommate's empty bed.

"Where is she?" I asked.

"With her son in the waiting room. Talk!"

We gave her the short version but she wanted details. I watched her face as we talked, looking for—I don't know—some sign of dread, of fear, some signal that meant "Stop, I don't mean it." *Something.* But I didn't see it. Maybe it was there, but I didn't see it. Nor did Ed. I kept asking him about it. I asked him that day, I had asked him the previous day, I asked him in the days that followed. It became a kind of ritual, on the order of "Do you really love me?" "Do you think she really wants to do it?" I'd say. I almost never said "kill herself." I would have liked to. Normally I am contemptuous of euphemism. But I had never needed euphemism the way I needed it now. Now the true words jammed, so I'd jump over them and land on "do it."

"Yes," Ed answered each time without a trace of impatience. He even said it in a whole sentence as he must have known I wanted him to. "Yes, I am convinced she really wants to do it. And even if she changes her mind, she should still be *able* to do it and she should *know* that she's able to do it."

We made one tactical error in giving my mother our detailed report. It was folly to have mentioned the time of the phone calls to Amsterdam. It was the only part of our recitation that seemed to distress her. "Three o'clock in the morning! And then eight o'clock! When did you sleep? You lost a whole night's sleep! No wonder," addressed to me, "you have circles under your eyes. Look what I'm doing to my children!"

Waiting for my mother to stop when she got on a tack like this was like standing in a doorway during a thundershower. Wait long enough and eventually it stops raining. Eventually she stopped talking, but not before emitting one small, unexpected blast of thunder. "I'll tell you one thing and this is definite," she said. "I don't want you to be there. I want to do it alone."

This stunned us both. We simply hadn't thought about that part of it; she was way ahead of us. How like her. How predictable, really. This was the woman, after all, who set the table for Saturday's party on Thursday. Of course she'd be plotting this. Until just now she hadn't known the menu, but that hadn't stopped her from making up the guest list. "I'm not having Shany there, either. I'm afraid she might try to stop me."

Ed and I sat at the foot of her bed, dumbfounded. She was going too fast for us. Ed broke the silence: "Ida," he said in his quiet, firm way, "I'll sit with you." My mother shook her head.

"What do you mean?" I said finally. "We'll both be there. Don't be ridiculous, Mother! Do you think we would—"

"Look," said Ed, putting up his hands to silence us both, "we can argue about this some other time. We don't have what we need yet, remember? That's what we should be thinking about now. We need a prescription from Dr. Goldman."

"Why can't I just ask him for it?" said my mother.

"Now?" Ed and I looked at her. Ahead of us again.

"Why not?" she went on. "I'm going home tomorrow. It's a perfect time. He always prescribes medication for me before I leave the hospital. So he can add one more. Where are my glasses? Here they are. Sweetheart, give me a piece of paper and a pencil. I want to write down the name of it. Nebu . . ."

"Nembutal," I whispered. She wrote it down. "Now give me the phone," she said, "and look in that drawer. I have Dr. Goldman's office number written down in a little notebook. There it is." She dialed the number and waited for him to come to the phone. Then she began her performance.

"Fine, I'm fine. Well, I'm not fine, but I'm better, much better, yes. . . . Yes, I'm looking forward to getting home. . . . Dr. Goldman, would you be a dear?" Here, just for a moment, her voice rose in pitch and sounded actressy. "I seem to have quite a bit of trouble sleeping lately, and I wondered if before I went home you could prescribe something a little stronger for me. I'll tell you, once before when I had this problem a doctor prescribed something wonderful." She lifted the paper in front of her face. "Nem-bu-tal, that was the name of it. Would you be a dear and write me out a prescription for some of that?"

I reached for my husband's hand and locked all of my fingers in his.

"Oh great, thanks so much. Fine. Yes. Tomorrow is fine."

She handed me the telephone receiver as if I were a secretary and she were a movie producer who had just closed a major deal. In a markedly different—darker—voice from the one she had used on the phone, she said, "He'll have a prescription ready for me before I leave."

Suddenly we heard a noise. We turned around to see

the roommate shuffling in on her son's arm. "Oh, I hope I'm not interrupting anything," she said.

"Not at all, dear," said my mother, brightening up again. "Not at all. We were just making some plans for tomorrow. I've always liked to plan, haven't I, sweetheart?" said my mother—actress, producer, chairman of the board, commander in the field.

19

chapter

October 10. We had won the dispute about being there when she took the pills. It wasn't much of a fight; she must have wanted—understandably—to lose.

That evening I flew to Boston. "Nightline" had given me an assignment to do a story on children's reactions to the possibility of nuclear war. Some schools in Boston were teaching classes on the subject and I guess it was controversial. I hardly remember. All I know is that they told me it would only take a day. I had dragged my feet on child abuse—it finally got finished, no thanks to me—and now that my mother's plan (I still didn't use the word, even in my own head) was probably going to come off soon, I'd be turning down the next assignment. So I thought I'd better do this one.

I don't know why I wasn't more worried about losing my job. True, my job did not require showing up at the office much. Mostly, it was a matter of being called at home for specific assignments. That made it easier not to be missed. Still, the producer of the show did expect me to come up with story ideas—I always had in the past—and also to display some kind of reportorial verve now and then. It must have been obvious, even when I appeared at the office, that I was there, as they say, in body only.

Almost no one at work knew about my mother's sickness, and even if they had, a sick mother is hardly an excuse for shirking work. Perhaps I hid my disengagement from work better than I thought.

As for not worrying about it, I attribute that to a simple shortage of space. My worry vat was filled. No room to fret about the consequences of shortchanging ABC News. As simple as that: no room.

The nuclear fear piece turned out pretty well, again no thanks to me. It was just one of those stories where everything rolls. The kids were good, as kids usually are. And the producer was one of the new, young, female, take-charge variety. I happily let her.

The day I went to Boston, Ed and Shany took my mother home from the hospital. While we were shooting in one of the classrooms, I slipped out and called Ed from the principal's office.

"I got it," he said, meaning the Nembutal. "And let me tell you, it wasn't easy. I had to go to three drugstores. It must be strong stuff." Suddenly he laughed. "You'll never guess what your mother got upset about."

"I give up. What?"

"It's raining, and when she found out I had to run

around to get the prescription filled, she started worrying that I'd get a cold."

"Did you have an umbrella?"

Another laugh. "You're your mother's daughter."

"I better get back to nuclear war."

"How's it going?"

"Okay, I guess. I'm not exactly concentrating."

"Well, concentrate. Everything's fine here. We've got what we need, your mother's fairly comfortable. Go to work."

"Yessir. Hey, sir?"

"What now?"

"I love you."

"I love you too. Now work!"

That night I called Shany. "There's one thing I don't understand," she said. "Your mother's all of a sudden in a good mood. She didn't bark at me once today."

"I hope you're not complaining."

She laughed a little. "No, but I just wonder. She seems so calm, like nothing bothers her."

"That's good," I said.

"I guess so," she said, not sounding sure.

October 12. I flew back to New York and went straight to my mother's apartment from the airport. Belva opened the door. We still had a nurse coming for the overnight shift, but my mother had insisted on getting Belva back during the day. She said it didn't matter that Belva couldn't give shots because the only time she had pain and needed a shot was at night.

When I arrived I found my mother sitting up at the big dining table in the living room. The table was too big for the apartment, but she had bought it in 1947—on it she had served hundreds of holiday and birthday dinners—and when moving time came she couldn't let it go. Now its top was virtually hidden under small piles of papers, envelopes, and folders. My mother, her glasses lodged near the end of her nose, was writing on some of them, stacking others.

"I'm getting some things in order," she said, barely looking up. "There's so much to do! I thought I had done it all, but I hadn't. Your mother is not organized the way she used to be. Remember how organized I used to be? Bills paid on the first of the month? I could never stand to look at an unpaid bill. To me an unpaid bill was an accusation." Then in a whisper, "Ask Belva if she wants to get out for a while."

I asked and Belva left, swiftly and silently as always.

As soon as the door closed, my mother began speaking faster. "This is a check for the November rent, so you know that is taken care of. Now the important thing is, the bearer bonds in my vault have to be moved into your vault. I'm going to tell you how to do that. It's very simple . . ."

Somewhere between the bearer bonds and the next item of business, I tuned out. I tried not to, but I was distracted by what I saw. What I saw, eyes pinned on me over the top of her glasses, was my mother, my vigorous, indefatigable, bossy, lovable mother, the one who led games in our Clark Street backyard, the one who made me sit straight while I practiced the piano. The mother, too, who ran a tight ship in Joe Brooks's construction company and who had bought real estate at the right time. The mother who nagged everyone in the world whom she loved to eat wheat germ. ("Once a day! A spoonful in your cereal! You won't even taste it.") I saw my mother and I realized, if she dies now she'll have never grown old. The thought struck me so forcibly—first as wonderful, then as terrible, then as wonderful again—that it was all I could do to keep from dropping to my knees and putting my head in her lap and crying my eyes out.

But I didn't do that. I wouldn't have dreamed of interrupting her when she was talking business. Instead I sat still and tried to pay attention.

Before I left I asked to see the capsules. Sure, she said, directing me without looking up from her papers to the place she had them hidden—under the embroidered guest towels in the back of the linen closet. I found them with my fingers and brought the bottle out under the light. Carefully I unscrewed the top and peered inside. When I saw them, I gasped. They were shiny, yellowish gelatin capsules, no bigger, each one, than a kernel of corn. "Oh" was all I said, but my mother must have read my mind.

"Small aren't they?" she said. "It'll be easy."

20

chapter

That night we set the alarm again and placed another call to Amsterdam. The closer we got to the countdown, the more new questions kept coming up. I had noted them. How long will it take for the pills to work? What should we do if she wakes up? Whom should we call when it's over?

Between five and six hours was the answer to the first question. To the second, "Keep her in bed. Make sure she doesn't get up and walk around. The dosage is strong enough to make it extremely unlikely that she would move, but if she did, it would happen within the first hour or two, and if she got up she could fall and hurt herself.

Then you'd be faced with a situation where you might have to get her to a hospital, and that's something you want to avoid." To the third question, about whom to call, the answer was her doctor rather than the police. "I don't know what the system is in New York when someone dies at home, but it's best to let the doctor know and have him tell you what to do next. He may instruct you to call the police. If so, that's what you should do. If everything goes smoothly, the doctor will write on the death certificate that your mother died of natural causes. If there's a suspicion of suicide there'll be an investigation. You don't want that."

I felt the words *you don't want that* in the soft center of my stomach. *You don't want that* got me thinking about what I hadn't thought about since the beginning, what I still didn't want to think about—that we were probably about to commit a crime. Ed had the same thought, I know, because when I reported to him the conversation with Amsterdam in its entirety, he said, "We have to be very careful." He said it in a low voice, but it echoed like a scream.

"Yes," I said, and looked at him, standing near the window in his bathrobe, his face pale, his hair falling in his eyes. My husband, as good and as honorable a man as there ever was, a man who won't deduct the cost of a book from his income tax unless it's a math book. If I had half the character he had, I thought as I looked at him, I would have kept him out of this. But I didn't. So I hadn't.

From then on we only spoke about the plan when we had to, and we spoke about it to no one but each other and Amsterdam, and when we did our voices were low and our words were few. And we never spoke about it using the real words. Everything was made doubly strange and tense by the holding pattern we seemed suddenly to be in.

My mother had the pills. She could have taken them at any time. But she didn't.

"Why isn't she doing it?" I asked Ed in bed the morning after the last Amsterdam call.

"I don't know."

"Could it mean she doesn't really want to?"

"It could," Ed said, his eyes on the ceiling, seeing nothing, I knew, without his glasses.

October 13. Thursday. There was still a lot of planning to do, more than I had expected. That as much as anything accounted for the delay. In a way the days that followed reminded me of the week of our wedding. We three had planned that too. It wasn't a grand wedding, but once Ed and I had decided not to go the judge's chambers route, each decision made seemed to lead to scores of others. No sooner had we chosen a place for the reception than we had to make a series of subdivided choices about the food and the music and the flowers and the so on and the so forth and, as I recall, our emotions were no more in sync with the nature of that occasion than with this one. We were so busy planning the wedding that we almost forgot that when it was over we'd be married. A kind of numbness set in. Maybe we wanted to be numb. Then, as now, the numbness calmed us. My mother, whose rapture about this union went off the top of the graph, grew increasingly like a bookkeeper at year's end. Whether profits or losses, the numbers had to tally. To look at her, then and now, was to know that they would.

We sat on her sofa like the three monkeys, my mother in the middle, a calendar opened on her lap. Belva had gone out on one of her enforced walks. "Belva dear, it's such a nice day," my mother would say in her Gracie

Allen voice, even if it was raining. "Why don't you get some fresh air?" And dear Belva would have her arms in her coatsleeves as soon as she heard the words *nice day.*

My mother tapped her pencil on *October.* We were in the process of picking a date. "Let's see," she said, "today is Thursday, the thirteenth. Too late for the bank today. What about tomorrow?" She looked at Ed.

"I won't be here tomorrow, Ida. There's a math conference in Washington. I promised to give a paper."

My mother looked pleased. "Oh, how nice," she said. "I have such smart children. Well then, the bank will have to wait until Monday. That means I won't do anything until Tuesday."

Tuesday! I thought, she *can't* wait that long! What if . . .

"What is it you want me to do at the bank?" said Ed.

"I want you to go to the vault and get those bearer bonds and put them into your vault in your bank. I want you to empty out whatever's there."

"Why now?" I asked.

"Because when people die they put a freeze on their vaults. They won't let you in for weeks, maybe even months."

"So what?" I said. "Who cares about that?"

"I care. I want you to get those things out of there. I don't want you to have to wait."

"Mother, what's the difference if we wait?" I didn't mean to raise my voice, but I did. Ed put his hand up. He could see she was getting agitated. No more, by now, than I. Tuesday, I thought, is five days from now. Lying on our backs in bed that morning we had considered, then decided against, Ed's canceling his Washington trip. For him to cancel and for her to suddenly die the same day might look suspicious, I thought. But now this vault business meant putting it off until next week! What if her digestion takes a bad turn? But I said nothing. I didn't want her even to think about her digestion.

"I'm not going to take those pills until you empty that vault," she said.

I almost laughed. "Mother! Are you threatening me? Please," I said quietly, folding my hand, "you don't have to do that. If you want us to go to the vault, we'll go to the vault. By the way, why can't *I* go tomorrow, without Ed I mean."

She shook her head. "Ed knows exactly what to do. They'll need your signature, but he should be there. Besides," (real reason) "it's dangerous. Walking around with bearer bonds is like walking around with cash."

"But I won't walk around. I'll take a taxi."

She shook her head. "I think I'll lie down now."

Ed helped her stand and walked her over to the bed. There's no point, I thought, in arguing about this. Her mind's made up. But I still didn't get it. She must have understood the risk in not acting now. I remembered what our friend from Amsterdam had said about people not going through with it. Putting it off until Tuesday might be her way of putting it off, period.

I sighed, feeling the usual split—half wanting it, half not wanting it. And over the split, an icing of unreality; I still couldn't believe she'd do it. Part of the incredibility of it all was that she didn't seem *that* sick. She seemed, not healthy certainly, but not agonized. I had to keep reminding myself that pain, up to a certain high level, is invisible and, more to the point, that her pain and discomfort would certainly get worse. Much worse.

"What time of day?" she asked.

I must have looked blank. Ed turned to me. "Your mother is asking what time of day she should take the pills."

"It's up to you, Mother," I said, sitting up straight. "What about afternoon?" I looked at her now. She was lying on top of her bed, her robe and slippers still on. "Are you comfortable?" I asked. "Don't you want to get into bed?"

"I'm fine. How would that work, then? Explain to me again what the doctor in Amsterdam said."

"He said you should have a little something to eat around six hours before, and then nothing. So you could have breakfast and—"

"What about Belva? We'd have to get her to leave."

"That shouldn't be a problem. I could just come over around five and tell her to go home early."

"Wouldn't that be suspicious ... afterwards?" my mother asked.

"I don't think so. Do you, Ed?"

Ed shook his head. "I assume you mean, will it look as if this was something we did to you? I don't think we have to worry about that. Or do you mean you don't want anyone to know what *you* did, Ida?"

"I'm not sure what I mean," said my mother. "What about the overnight nurse?"

"We can cancel her."

"That *will* look suspicious."

"No, it won't. We can just tell her we're getting another nurse."

"Why would we all of a sudden get a new nurse?" my mother said.

"I don't know. It doesn't matter. We can just say we're going back to using aides at night. She knows you've been better lately."

"What about afterwards? Won't it look suspicious if no one was here?"

"Not if you do the canceling. No one can prove we knew you canceled."

Silence from my mother. That seemed to go down.

"I want you to leave as soon as possible—right after. I really don't like your being here at all."

"Mother," I said, "we've been over that a hundred times. We're going to be here. We're not going to *do* anything, but we'll be here."

There was still some question about when we should leave. Ed and I had talked about it over breakfast that morning, and as we walked home that evening we talked about it again. The doctor had said that if she didn't digest the pills, if there was going to be trouble, we'd know it pretty soon, either right away or within the first hour or two. After that, we could assume that her digestive system had done its job. At the end of that last conversation he had advised me against waiting around.

"Leave the building—and be seen by the doorman— and return the next day," he added. "Or have someone *else* find her the next day. Should there be an investigation, it's better if, at some point during the period when she might have swallowed the capsules, you two weren't around. Then there would be no way of proving she didn't do it herself. Do you understand?"

I didn't totally understand and I didn't want to. I didn't want to think about afterwards at all. I almost *couldn't* think about it, as if something physical prevented it, like a sudden impairment of vision. Yesterday I could see beyond that lamppost and today I can't. Today beyond that lamppost is a blur.

On our walk home we decided—ashamedly, guiltily, helplessly—that Belva had to be the one to find her. Belva would come to work Wednesday morning as usual and she would discover that during the night her patient had died. Not to do it that way would mean canceling her in advance, which surely would make her wonder. And how could we know what she would do? We couldn't know.

We loved her, but like Shany we couldn't trust her not to act.

"I guess in that line of work you probably see people expire now and then. It surely won't be her first time."

"I'm sure it won't," Ed said.

"It's still a rotten thing to do, isn't it?"

"I'm not sure if it is or not. But I don't think we have a lot of choice."

We crossed Fifth Avenue and headed west. It was twilight, a beautiful, clear fall evening. The streets were full of dressed-up strollers who looked merrier than they probably were. On the corner of Fifty-fifth Street, three raggle-taggle musicians were playing "When the Saints Go Marching In."

"I just thought of something," I said, shouting over the saxophone. "When Belva gets there in the morning there'll be no nurse. Won't she wonder why? Of course she will, especially if she finds my mother—"

"Maybe," Ed shouted back. Then in a lower voice, "But remember what you just told your mother. How does Belva know your mother didn't cancel the nurse herself? Anyway, whatever she thinks it'll be over by then, and I don't really think Belva is interested in getting us locked up."

"I don't either. Still, it's bound to make her think something funny is going on." We were in the block now, past the music and most of the people. "We're going to have to tell her something. She walks in, no one's there, and my mother's dead. She's going to wonder."

I had said the word. *Dead.* I felt proud of myself. I waited to see if I felt anything; I didn't. We walked faster. "We'll just have to tell her—in advance—that the night nurse is leaving early and might be gone in the morning by the time she gets there and not to worry."

"How will Belva get into the apartment?"

We were at our building now. I smiled at the doorman. "She has a key, at least I think she does. I'll check."

When we got inside our apartment I pulled off my shoes, and with my coat still on, leaned against the wall, and just for a moment, closed my eyes. "You know what this experience has taught me?"

"No, what?" asked my husband, removing my coat from my arms as if I were a child in a snowsuit.

"New respect for the intelligence of criminals."

Ed had grown uncommonly silent during the last few days. He did his computations, taught his classes, kept his life on its customary path, but he spoke less and ate less.

Come to think of it, so did I. My mother noticed. "You're getting too thin," she had told me earlier in the week. I'm not sure why, but when she said this I began to cry. That is I let myself cry. I could have cried at any moment of any day during the last days, but I didn't because I thought if I cried it might be hard to stop and I didn't want to spend energy that way. And I especially didn't want to cry in front of my mother, because I thought surely that would get *her* going. Common sense told me that the only way we would all get through this thing was to keep the group temperature down. On the other hand, I didn't want to turn into a robot, and I didn't want my mother to think that I had.

But this is Monday morning quarterbacking. As one tear made its way down one cheek and another down the other, I had no idea—no conscious idea—of why I allowed their passage.

"Please, sweetheart, don't be upset," my mother said. "I'm doing what I want to do. I don't feel the least bit sorry for myself. I'm lucky I can get out of this. The people I feel sorry for are all the people who want to and can't. Please, sweetheart."

I wiped my face with the back of my hand. "I know what you're saying, Mother, and I agree with you. But you can't expect me not to be upset. I think it's right what you're doing, but—but I love you. How can I not be upset?"

She listened quietly when I said that. With some unsteadiness, I got up and blew my nose and came back and sat down. Then we resumed our plotting.

21

chapter

OctZZZber 14. Ed went off to his conference and I took the bus up to ABC. It was strange being in the office. The normalcy of the place struck me like a sudden temperature change. "Nightline" had a young staff, but they seemed even younger than I remembered. Younger and breezier. I noticed I was breezy back.

More and more, lately, I found myself noticing things about myself, as if I had stepped outside my skin and were looking in. The person I saw when I did that often seemed mechanically run, as if she had a key in her back. Self-winding of course.

I called my mother from the office. She expected her friend Rose, she said, and later Shany and how are you, sweetheart. She sounded light, very light and airy. I listened hard for another kind of sound, but I didn't hear it. Or maybe the wind-up soldier I had become didn't hear it. Ed said no; later on when he called her, then me, from Washington, Ed said that he didn't hear it either.

I didn't stay in the office long. A few people had ordered in Chinese food and the smell was making me queasy. On my way out, one of the producers told me about a "neat" assignment he and I had for next week—to do a piece on the one hundredth anniversary of the Metropolitan Opera. We could start shooting Tuesday morning, he said. "I've got Pavarotti lined up for Tuesday afternoon."

I'm awfully sorry, I thought. Tuesday won't be convenient. Tuesday is the day my mother is planning to kill herself. "That sounds great," I said. "Let's, uh, talk tomorrow."

It's strange having a secret, at least it is for me. I tend to tell things. It's a way of connecting with people. Not telling has the opposite effect and I don't like it. I was beginning to feel more and more cut off from everyone, except of course from the few people, countable on one hand with fingers to spare, who knew. To those people I felt an extreme connection, as if by electrical wire. To my husband I felt fused.

Over the weekend my mother received more visitors— not including Alvin, although they still spoke every day on the telephone. Elaine came and brought her wonderful noodle pudding, Shany came and chain-smoked, and her brother came and told her about a cure for cancer he had just read about and why didn't she look into it. And late Saturday afternoon an old friend from Yonkers, Emma Goldin, came on her way to the airport. I ran into her in the lobby as she was leaving. Her eyes were red and she hugged me. She said that she had told my mother she wanted to pray for her and asked my mother what the prayer should be. "Pray that by the time you come back from your trip I'll be gone," my mother had said.

I didn't stay long. I was afraid I might thaw if I did. I was nicely frozen and I wanted to stay that way. As for my mother, she seemed normal—almost unbelievably normal. She talked, she laughed, she listened. I didn't know what to make of it. Not that I tried.

Going down in the elevator I ran into someone else I knew, a German Jewish woman named Frieda who was about my age and who lived in the building. I had met her years ago through a childhood friend, Karen. When I first saw Frieda in the building a month or so earlier, I remembered her only slightly, but one fact of her life stuck in my mind—both of her parents had died in Auschwitz. She had spent most of her life as a nomad, living alternately in Europe and the United States, working at this job and that, never quite settling into anything or settling down with anyone. She was a pretty woman—rather elegant, I thought—with blondish, swept-back hair and deep, gray-green eyes.

"How's your mother?" Frieda said, and something about the way she said it made me feel she really wanted to know.

"Not good," I answered.

"I'm sorry," she said, again as if she meant it. "If there's anything I can do, *anything*, please call on me. I mean that sincerely."

"I know you do," I said, "and perhaps I will. Thank you. Thank you very much."

Ed returned from his math conference in Washington and that evening we went to Carnegie Hall. Ann Reinking, the dancer, was performing in a one-woman show.

We had complimentary tickets, which I had planned to send back, but didn't. Then it got to be Saturday and, given my mother's excess of company, we decided to go.

I aimed my eyes straight ahead at the stage and they stayed there. My thoughts were less obedient. They rose in the air and floated out of sight like a lost balloon. I kept thinking, in particular, of one piece of the plan we had not yet worked out. How were we going to find someone to sit with my mother as she moved from unconsciousness to death? Given that the good doctor from Amsterdam had warned us not to linger in my mother's apartment after a couple of hours—even though she wouldn't die for at least five hours—the problem was that we didn't want to leave her alone as long as she was still alive. The doctor had assured us that the chance of her stirring after a couple of hours was virtually nil and not to worry about leaving her alone. That sounded reasonable, but I couldn't imagine doing it; nor could Ed.

As Ann Reinking flew across the stage with her fine, long legs, I silently went over it all again. Even though the doctor had convinced me of the legal danger of our being there, I had a hard time taking the danger as seriously as he seemed to. Imagine anyone thinking Ed and I had murdered my mother. It sounded like a bad joke or an even worse television movie. Still, it scared me a little. Didn't people get locked up every day for crimes they didn't commit? And besides, were we not, in fact, committing a crime by helping her to kill herself? I still didn't know for sure and I still didn't want to.

There were several dancers on stage now, all in black, moving very stylishly in perfect synchronization. To be on the safe side (as my mother would have said), we had better leave her as the doctor advised and try to get someone to stay with her for a couple of hours or so, until it was over. But who? We had talked about this again on the walk to Carnegie Hall.

One of our trusted friends probably would have done it, but we both felt that would be leaning on a friend too hard. Still, if we couldn't ask a friend, whom *could* we ask? Anyone who did it would risk being seen entering and leaving the building and might, therefore, be questioned. It might be cops-and-robbers paranoia to expect any of this to happen. All the same . . .

And then it came to me. The first act had ended. Everyone was applauding, and as my hands rose automatically with theirs, I remembered Frieda, the woman in my mother's building. "Frieda!" I shouted to Ed over the applause. "We can get Frieda! Nobody would see her come or go! She lives in the building!" The people in the seats next to us were waiting for us to stand so they could get out. "Excuse me," we all said. Ed and I stood, then slid back down in our chairs.

"Maybe we could pay her," I said. Ed made a face. "She's awfully nice, but she's not really a friend and I'd want to do something in return."

"Does she need money?"

"I think she actually does."

Ed was silent for a moment. "Are you sure we can trust her?"

"Yes."

"Why?"

"I just am. Instinct. I'm sure. Besides, she's Karen's oldest friend."

I called Frieda Sunday morning, and asked her if I could stop by and see her for a moment that afternoon before I visited my mother. We made a date for four o'clock. Ed, meanwhile, went directly to my mother's. When I got to the building I deliberately didn't ask the doorman to ring Frieda's apartment. More cops and robbers. It was better, I figured, if there was no connection made between the two of us. I had by now lost track of when I was taking a sensible precaution and when I was being ridiculous. Better, I thought, to err on the side of being ridiculous.

I told Frieda straight out what I wanted, and she burst into tears. Which threw me, almost annoyed me. I had my mind on nuts and bolts and here she was, getting all feverish over the grand design. I sat on her small sofa, looked at her poster of Israel on the opposite wall, and waited for her to stop.

"I'm sorry," she said. "I couldn't possibly do such a thing. And if I could I certainly wouldn't want payment."

Her words said no, but something in her face said maybe not no. "Frieda, I'm afraid I've insulted you by mentioning money. It's just that you're not a close friend and it's a huge thing to ask and it is a task—a job, really. I didn't feel right asking you to do it without offering to pay you. In fact, if you did it, there would be no way to pay you sufficiently."

She wiped her eyes with a handkerchief. "What exactly would you want me to do?"

"To come to the apartment at about eight o'clock. We'd still be there. Then we'd leave and you'd stay for a few hours. It's extremely unlikely that anything would happen in those few hours, but if it did—if my mother tried to get up—you'd make sure she stayed in bed and didn't hurt herself. As I say, the chances of that happening are very, very small."

She got up and walked to the window. Turning away from me, she looked out. We were on a higher floor than my mother's apartment and the street noises were more distant. The car horns sounded almost ghostly. After ten or twenty seconds she turned back toward me and shook her head. "I'm sorry. I admire what your mother is doing. But I . . . can't."

I got up and put my arm around her shoulder. "Don't give it another thought," I said. "I understand. And I'm sorry if I upset you."

My mother was sitting up in the living room talking to Ed. She had on a frilly, flowered new bathrobe—a present from Elaine's daughter—and her cheeks were flushed. She looked almost merry. I sat down and turned around. "Where's Belva?"

"I sent her home early," my mother said. "I thought that would be a good idea. Then when Tuesday comes she won't think it's so strange."

Ed and I exchanged a look, this latest evidence of her shrewdness registering on both of us. In spite of my numbness, the way she talked about it still jarred me. She was too calm, too matter-of-fact. It almost made me think she didn't understand what she was about to do. It almost made me think she was crazy.

"Sweetheart," she said, "we might make a little change." I straightened up. "I was telling Ed, there's no point waiting until Tuesday. If you kids go to the vault tomorrow morning—that's really the only reason to wait—I can do it tomorrow afternoon."

I knew I was supposed to respond, but my brain and my larynx lost contact. Until I saw her tugging at her wedding ring. "What are you doing?"

"I want to give this to you. But—darn it—it won't come off. Betts, get me some hand lotion, will you? Over there on the bureau." I felt my weight shift to my legs. My legs moved to the bureau. I picked up the hand lotion and turned around. I watched the extension of my arm as

I gave it to her. She took the bottle from me, unscrewed the top, and put some lotion on her finger. Another pull and the ring slipped off. She handed it to me as if it were a coin for the laundromat. "Here. Put it in your bag."

I pressed my lips together and swallowed and kept swallowing. I put the ring in a zipper compartment in my bag. She looked at her finger and rubbed it. "You know," she said to Ed, "I think that's the first time I've taken that ring off since I put it on. That's fifty-one or fifty-two years? We were married in 1931, so we would have had our fifty-second wedding anniversary last May—is that right?"

"Fifty-two is right," said Ed.

My mother smiled. "It's nice to have a mathematician in the family.

"Sweetheart," she said, turning to me now, "don't look sad. Your mother is doing exactly what she wants to do. Do you know how grateful I am that I can get out of this? Do you think I want to wait until somebody has to pull a plug? Believe me, I'm the happiest woman in the world that I can do this. But to do it alone—I admit it—that would have been much harder. This way, with my children near me ... But what mother has such children? Name one mother who ..."

She was off and running, but quickly doubled back for a final strategy session. She wanted to set exact times for everything: nine-thirty for our trip to the bank; ten for my arrival at her apartment to tell her the deed was done; four-thirty for my later arrival at her apartment; four-forty-five for Belva's departure; five for Ed's arrival (he'd be coming straight from school); five-forty-five for the Compazine; six for the pills. She began to write the schedule down. Then she thought better of it, tore up the piece of paper, and ran through the schedule again on her fingers, holding them up one at a time as she ticked off the steps.

Ed asked her if she had seen Shany today. She nodded slowly, guiltily. None of us liked deceiving Shany, my mother least of all. She kept reconsidering, but then she'd shake her head. "I just can't take the chance," she'd say. "I can't take the chance." Ed had an idea about Shany, though, which my mother brightened to at once. She could write Shany a note. We handed her her stationery and a pen.

"What'll I say?" This to me. Questions about numbers went to Ed; I got the ones about words.

"That you want to do what you're doing," I said, "and that you love her." My mother nodded, wrote, sealed the envelope, and handed it to me. "I think I'd like to go back to bed now." We each took an arm and helped her across the room. She lay back on the pillow and closed her eyes. "I wish it were over," she whispered.

"It will be soon," I said, taking her hand.

"What do people do who don't have children?" she said looking up at me. "What if you want to get out and you have no one to help you?"

"Mother, you look so tired. Why don't you take a nap. We'll sit here until the nurse comes." She nodded and turned over on her side. I pulled the covers up around her shoulders and turned out the light.

"Betts?"

"Yes?" I turned around in the doorway.

"Are you going to write about this?"

The question stunned me—not because I hadn't thought of it, but because I hadn't expected *her* to. "Is that what you want?"

"Yes," she said. I stood in the dark for a moment, then tiptoed out. She was already asleep.

* * *

When I opened the door for the night nurse I noticed
an envelope on the floor. I picked it up and read my name.
Inside was a single piece of paper with a handwritten
note: "I'll do it. Frieda." I folded the paper and put it in
my purse with the ring.

22

chapter

October 17. My mother's vault was in a small branch of the Chemical Bank on Fifty-sixth Street and First Avenue, a few blocks from her apartment. She had a neighbor's kind of friendship with the man who presided over the vault area. He was a small, elderly Italian who matched exactly my memory of our grocer in Yonkers—the sort who falls all over himself trying to be helpful; the sort too, I could tell right away, whose life story my mother would have mined at each clip of her coupons.

"How's Mom doin'?" he asked.

"Not very well," I said.

His face literally fell. "Oh, I'm sorry to hear that. She's

a lovely lady, your mom, a lovely lady." Then he smiled. "And the apple doesn't fall far from the tree."

"Thank you," I said, and to both his astonishment and my own, my lip started to quiver.

"He caught me off guard," I explained to Ed as we walked outside. "He was so corny and sweet. He reminded me of her. I suddenly *missed* her as if ... and she's not even ..."

"Take it easy," Ed said, holding me around the shoulders as we walked down the block. "This day has only just begun."

He needn't have warned me. I knew. The slippage at the bank helped, though. It reminded me to take more care to keep myself emotionally tidy—corners swept, covers pulled tight. I knew if I got messy the whole plan could go awry. I could imagine it all too easily: I get upset, she gets upset, her digestion goes, she throws up the pills and winds up back in her cell.

"I am going to be calm," I vowed to Ed as we approached my mother's apartment. "I am going to be calm." Following her instructions, Ed dropped me off and went on to our bank to put the contents of her vault in ours.

"Oh, I'm glad to see you, Miss Rollin," said Belva when I got upstairs. "I need a few things from the market, and now that you're here I can go out and get them."

I didn't believe her, which made me all the more grateful. Before this day got under way, I wanted time alone with my mother. As soon as the door closed, I sat down on the foot of my mother's bed and searched her face the way I had searched it every day for the past two weeks, straining still to see the crack, the signal—any signal—to stop. Ed kept saying there was no reason to look so closely because we weren't driving, she was. "We're only navigators, remember. And at this point she knows the way herself. That means if she doesn't want to go, all she has to do is not go. We're not doing anything to encourage her one way or the other. I think we've been very careful not to do that."

We had indeed been careful not to do that. I still made it a rule never to bring the subject up with her, never to say a word about it until she said a word first. Which she always did.

"How was your night?" I said.

"Not bad. Did Ed make the deposit?"

"He's on his way."

"Did he take a taxi?"

"Yes."

"Will he call me after it's done?"

"You asked him to. I'm sure he will."

"I'm sure he will too," she said and leaned back on the pillow and shook her head slowly back and forth. "I must have done something good in my life to be blessed with him." She sounded sad the way she did sometimes when the weight of some happiness or other made her sink a little. "Do you know how grateful I am for this marriage of yours?"

"No," I said with the sarcasm of normal times. "Tell me."

"It means I can die in peace. Do you know what it means for a mother to leave her only child knowing she's taken care of? I don't mean material things, you know that. I mean a good person who loves you and whom you love. I always wanted that for you and now you have it. Do you have any idea how that makes me feel? How many mothers can die with such joy?"

"Mother," I said, holding myself still, "I hope you don't think . . . you have to go through with this. You are not obliged to go through with this, Mother. I hope you know that."

She looked at me as if I had gone around the bend. "*Obliged?* Obliged to whom? I can't wait! I had such pain last night." She shook her head back and forth on the pillow. "The shot helped, but even before the shot I didn't mind because I thought, I'm getting out of this. Someone else might feel differently. I've told you I don't think for a minute that what I'm going through is worse than what a lot of people suffer who want to live. Believe me, I know what people go through. Look at your cousin Honey, how she suffered and how she hung on. But that was different. She wasn't even fifty yet. Her children weren't grown. Poor Honey, of course she hung on. But what's that got to do with me? What do I need to hang on for? For what? Life has given me everything I wanted. Seventy-six wonderful years—how many people can say that?—but now it's over. I thank God my brain is still working so that I know it's over. And I thank God I can swallow right now so that I can get out." She smiled. "It's almost enough to make me religious."

"Aren't you religious?" Even as I spoke, I knew it was a first date question. And although I had never asked it, I knew the answer.

"No."

"But you . . . mention God a lot. You always have. You just did."

"I know. I guess I believe there's something. But I don't know what it is. I don't think anyone knows. It's hard sometimes, because I need someone to thank. So I thank God; who else should I thank for my wonderful children?" Her eyes moved past me and scanned the room. "Sweetheart, don't move the furniture out before you sell the apartment. People have no imagination. You'll do better if it's furnished. Believe me. Your mother knows what she's talking about."

The phone rang. Shany. "Fine, fine," my mother said.

"Betty's here. Yes, tomorrow's fine. I'll see you tomorrow." She hung up and lay back on the pillow. "Whew. I forgot that Shany might come today. You know something, I better make sure." She picked the phone up again and dialed Shany's number. "Listen, I thought I better tell you in case you change your mind or something, Alvin may come this afternoon. . . . Well, I thought I'd let him come, so tomorrow really is better. Okay? Good, see you tomorrow." Then to me, "She'll never come if she thinks Alvin will be here."

"Have you seen Alvin?"

She shook her head no. "We talk on the phone. That's enough."

Alvin, I thought. He'll be devastated. Can't worry about Alvin, though, can't . . .

The phone rang again. Ed this time, reporting the vault deposit. "Good," my mother said as she hung up. "That's done. Now who's going to stay here after you leave?"

I hoped she had forgotten. I didn't like talking to her about afterwards and I had begun to think she didn't want to hear about it. I sighed and told her about Frieda, keeping it short. As usual, she wanted to know more. In no time she got it out of me that Frieda's parents had died in a concentration camp. "Oh, how terrible," she gasped. "What a shame I didn't know her. A girl like that, alone—I could have had her to dinner, helped her out. Why didn't you ever introduce her to me?"

"I hardly know Frieda, Mother. She's an old friend of Karen's, but I never got to know her well myself."

My mother frowned. "I feel bad I didn't help her. And now look what she's doing for me."

Belva returned, announcing herself with a gentle tapping on the door. It was eleven o'clock. My mother said she wanted to nap and suggested I leave and come back later, at around four or four-thirty.

I was glad to leave. Outside, the air slapped my cheeks. It felt good. I shoved my hands in the pockets of my jacket and began walking automatically in the direction of my apartment. When I got to the corner I stopped. It occurred to me that I had no reason to go home, so instead I turned right and went up Third Avenue, then left to Park, then up Park. I looked around me as I walked. It was Monday morning. Everyone looked purposeful, heads up, faces flushed, briefcases swinging. With my running shoes on, I too moved at a good clip, but I didn't feel as if I were moving at all. I didn't even feel that I was there. Or anywhere. At the corner of Sixty-third Street I stopped and turned around. I decided, for no particular reason, to go home after all.

When I got upstairs I called Ed. He reported that he had just spoken to her. "She sounds fine," he said.

"Do you think so?"

"Yes. Don't you?"

"I guess. You don't think she's acting?"

"No, I don't."

"You think she really wants to do this?"

"Yes, I do."

When we hung up I looked down at my appointment book. "October 17," it said. "12:30: Hair. Kenneth." I looked at the clock: twelve-ten. I ran my fingers through my hair and I tried to remember when I had last washed it. Looking again at the clock, I considered: Does a sane person go to the beauty parlor five and a half hours before her mother kills herself? I knew the answer, but I wanted to go anyway. It had nothing to do with my hair. I just wanted to be there. Kenneth is a very nice place to be. I wanted to sit in a flowered smock among the pedicures and the hair driers and float for an hour.

I got there in fifteen minutes. And I floated. The hair-dresser—Glenn was his name—put me on a high chair, one of those chairs that make you feel you are sitting on top of a cake. Glenn chatted at me. I chatted back. A uniformed woman with perfect manners brought me a cup of coffee in a pink-flowered china cup. The temperature of the coffee was—like that of Goldilocks' porridge—just right. Then, too soon, it was over. In forty-five minutes I was out on the street again.

I went back home. I took my coat off, hung it up more carefully than necessary, and sat down on a chair in the living room. I got up and sat down on a chair in the bedroom. I looked at the telephone. I picked it up. I dialed my mother's number.

"Just checking in," I said.

"I'm fine, sweetheart. I had lunch a little while ago. I'm fine."

"Do you want me to come earlier than four-thirty?"

"No, I don't think so. Four, four-thirty is fine."

Good, I thought. She feels the same way I do. It's better if we keep our distance today. Like a bride and groom on the day of the wedding.

I didn't want to stay in the apartment, though. So I called Joanna, a close friend who knew, and asked her if I could come by and have a cup of tea with her. Of course, she said, and mentioned a three o'clock appointment. "But that still gives us an hour together. And if you want to, Betty, you can stay in the apartment after I've left. In fact, why don't I just break my appointment. It's not important. I'll—"

I told her I'd come over only on the condition that she keep her appointment. She agreed. I ran part of the way and arrived at Joanna's out of breath. She hugged me, sat me down in her living room as if my eyesight were failing, and made tea for us both. I think I talked about the day so far—I remember Joanna saying sweet, sympathetic things back—and I must have mentioned Frieda because Joanna said that I should have asked *her* to sit with my mother, that she would have done it and would still if I wanted her to. I was moved by that, but I don't know if I showed it. I think I may have just sat there like a stone.

It came time for her to go. I decided to stay. When the door closed behind her, I went back into the living room and sat down facing the window. There were some magazines and newspapers on the coffee table. I picked up *House & Garden* and looked at pictures of an English country house. It was pretty—a lot of flowers. I put the magazine down and got up and walked to the window. A large building was under construction next door. I watched one of the workmen. He was near enough for me to see his face. A young face. Suddenly, with no warning, the picture flipped and I imagined him upside down, falling to the ground.

I turned from the window, sat back down, and picked up a *New York Times*. My eyes moved across some type on the front page which had to do with a new American-Canadian accord providing "for further cleansing of phosphorous pollutants in the Great Lakes. But," I read, "at a meeting in Halifax, Nova Scotia, United States and Canadian officials were still at odds over Washington's failure to propose a program for reducing acid rain in . . ."

I folded the paper carefully, placed it down on the coffee table, and stood up again. I walked across the room, looked at a small painting of a boat, and walked back and sat down and called Ed. He said his class was about to begin and he'd see me later. I hung up and stared at the rug. It was blue and white and faded in a nice way. I stood up and put on my jacket and walked into the kitchen and looked at the clock. Three-thirty-five.

I left the apartment and went out into the brightness and the traffic and the horns and the people on First Avenue. I walked uptown and looked in store windows. They were mostly dry cleaners and food stores—not the sort of windows you look into. I looked into them anyway. All Work Done on the Premises; Chicken Legs, 29¢ per lb. A crazy person with matted hair and many layers of clothing came lurching up the avenue. I avoided eye contact, as I've learned to do, but I felt a connection all the same. I crossed the avenue to the other side.

A clock in a coffee shop said three-forty-five. I walked faster. What if she was pretending on the phone and she's upset and she can't swallow? What if she swallows half the pills but can't get down the rest? The lid had slipped off the jar in my brain and the contents were spilling all over the avenue. What if she swallows them all and wakes up a vegetable? What if she starts throwing up before . . .

"Hello, Miss Rollin," said Belva in her sweet-shy way. "Your mother is just having a little rest now," she whispered. "She fell asleep about a half hour ago, so I expect she'll be up before too long."

"How has she been today?"

"Quite well today, Miss Rollin, quite well."

I waited for a *but.* Instead Belva turned and went into the kitchen and picked up her embroidery. I tiptoed into the bedroom. My mother was curled up on her side, facing the wall. I stood and watched the blanket move up and down as she breathed. After a minute or so, I turned toward the big table near the window and picked up the chart. The report of the night nurse was on top.

9 P.M. Dalmane, 30 mg   For sleep. Slept fairly well
12:30 A.M. Demerol, 1½ cc,   until 12 midnight. Took
   75mg   Demerol for pain. Had
                           good effect.

| 6:30 A.M. | Slept through until 6:30 A.M. |
| | Awake and TV on. Cheer-ful. |

The next entry was in Belva's handwriting:

8:30 A.M Mylanta, 1 T.	On arrival patient up and
11:50 Reglan, 1 T.	watching TV. Cheerful.
12:30 P.M. Mylanta, 1 T.	Had breakfast & bath.
	Visit from daughter.
	Back to bed. Slept until
	12:30. Had lunch, 1 egg
	& half English muffin.

My eyes doubled back to the word *cheerful*, then to the word *cheerful* again. Two *cheerfuls*. I put the chart down.

"Hello, sweetheart."

"Hi, Mother." I bent down and kissed her and straightened out her white cap, askew as it always was after a nap. "How about an extra hug?" she said. "My pleasure," I said and bent down again and hugged her—quickly, though. Hugs, I knew, were dangerous; they tapped feelings. I had learned that in an amateur acting class I once took. "If you don't have the feeling, *do* something and you'll find it will come," the teacher had said. "Jump up and down and you'll start feeling happier. Weep, and see if misery doesn't bob to the surface. Try it!"

I'll stay frozen, thank you.

"When is Ed coming?" my mother asked, sitting straight up. Her face seemed brighter, somehow, pinker, as if—

She was wearing makeup.

"Soon," I said when I found my voice. "In about a half hour."

"Good."

"Ed will help us . . . be calm."

"Oh Belva," my mother called. "My Betty is here now. Why don't you go home. You've had such a long day."

"Very well, Mrs. Rollin," said Belva, appearing at the doorway.

"By the way. Belva," I said. "The night nurse said she might have to leave early, so you can just let yourself in if she's gone. You . . . do have a key, don't you?"

"Oh yes. I can come early if you like, Miss Rollin."

"Oh, no," I said, perhaps a little too quickly. "That's . . . not necessary."

"Very well," said Belva. We did our good-byes the same as always, and she left.

I sat down in the chair next to my mother's bed and inhaled slowly. I thought about Elisabeth Kübler-Ross and her theories about "unfinished business"—about saying, before you die, all the things you've always held back. The thought almost made me smile. When had my mother ever held anything back? But surely there was something serious we should talk about now.

"Betts?"

"Yes?"

"There's a package in the closet from Bloomingdale's you should return. I think I paid about fifteen dollars for it. It's that headrest for the bathtub I bought for you one time and you told me you didn't want it. So make sure you take it back, okay?"

"Okay." She closed her eyes and I got up and walked to the window.

"Betts?"

"Yes, Mother?"

"There's another package in the linen closet. It's a present for the Freedman grandchild. Will you get it to him? It's a lovely book."

"I'll get it to him."

"Sweetheart?"

"Yes?"

"I love you."

The lump in my throat—the one that had been in residence for the past month—swelled suddenly. "I love you too, Mother."

Hold on, I warned myself. Hold on. Slowly, I came back and sat down on the bed and took her hand. There was an identation on her third finger where her wedding ring used to be.

She saw me looking at it and said, "I used to think Daddy was lucky to die the way he did, but I don't anymore. It's easier to go like that, but look what he missed. Look at the last year I had. It was worth the torture treatments."

"I'm glad you feel that way. I wasn't sure that you did."

"Of course I feel that way. Not with these last two chemotherapy treatments, though. They were just playing with me. They had to do something, so they figured they'd torture me a little." She sighed. "I think I'll close my eyes for a few minutes."

"That's a good idea." I stood and bent over her and kissed her on her forehead. The powder on her face gave off a faint smell of perfume.

"Sweetheart?"

"Yes, Mother."

"You'll pay Belva for the whole day tomorrow, won't you?"

"Of course I will." I began to walk out of the room and stopped. "Mother, did you cancel the overnight nurse?"

"Yes. Belva went out for some groceries, and while she was out I called."

My God, I thought, she's going to do it.

I walked into the living room and sat down at the piano. I touched the keys with the tips of my fingers, the white keys first, then the black ones, pressing them down but making no sound. I think I must not have heard Ed's tap on the door right away. When I did, it made me jump.

"Sorry," I whispered as I let him in. "I think she's sleeping." He nodded and put down his briefcase and hung up his trenchcoat. We sat down together in the living room, side by side, like parents.

"Is that my darling son?"

"Yes, Ida," Ed said, shooting up. "May I come in?"

"Of course," she said, and we both went into the bedroom. My eyes moved from the bed to the clock on her night table. Exactly five. My insides came together in what felt like one small, hard knot in the center of my body. It made me want to bend over. Instead, I sat—we both sat—on either side of the bed. Ed leaned over and kissed her on the cheek.

"Let's try to be normal and calm," I said, not more than half aware that the only person in the room who needed calming was me. With that, I turned on the television set. The local news had just begun. It was called "Live at Five." Ed gave me a look and turned it off.

My next impulse, though equally rooted in hysteria, had better results. "Why don't we get out some books of photographs?" I said and, without waiting for a reaction, charged into the living room and dragged from the bottom drawer of the mahogany breakfront five or six large photo albums. I laid one of them on the blanket over my mother's lap and opened it to the first page. For a moment she looked startled. Then, her eyes still on the page, she reached for her glasses. I turned on the bedside light. She smiled.

"That's Betty's first birthday party," she said to Ed,

pointing to a group picture of our family seated around a table. "Betty slept through most of it, but we had a wonderful time. There's Aunt Sarah, Uncle Harry, Shany. Look, there's Daddy in front of the Clark Street house. Oh, I remember those geraniums. They were the first geraniums I ever grew. I had a little victory garden in the back, too."

"I remember. You used to let me water it sometimes. I thought that was a big treat."

"We had a victory garden in Illinois," Ed said. "What did you grow in yours, Ida?"

"Oh, beans, tomatoes. The tomatoes were wonderful. You could take them in your hand and eat them like fruit. Look Ed, do you know who that is?" She pointed at a small photograph of my third grade Christmas pageant. "Who's he?" she said, putting her finger under one of the Wise Men, a skinny kid holding a staff.

"I give up," Ed said.

"It's Joel Goldin," my mother said with a little smile as she watched Ed's reaction. Joel Goldin is our dentist.

"I don't believe it. Wait a minute. Who's the other . . . I think that other Wise Man is my wife!"

"I wasn't going to say a word," I said. "Don't you love the baggy tights?"

"They are not baggy," my mother said. "I made that costume. Look, Ed, I made this one too." She pointed now to a photograph of me in a long white dress (not long enough to hide my huge feet) with stars and stripes on it. I wore a cardboard crown on my head, and stood surrounded by the other members of my sixth grade class, all of whom looked only slightly less miserable than I did. "Miss America," said my mother. "I stayed up all night sewing those stars and stripes." She shook her head. "It was a labor of love."

The next page held photographs of the house in Yonkers she had moved, along with a nicely preserved clipping from the Yonkers *Herald Statesman.* Ed read the headline out loud: "Her Home a Headache on Rollers." The story went on to say that my mother had no idea what would be involved in the move and that if she had to do it over again she would have "bought a house that would stay where it was."

"What baloney," my mother said. "I never said any such thing. That was the best idea I ever had and I knew it and so did everybody else." She turned around suddenly and looked at the clock on her night table. "Isn't it time?"

Isn't it time? She said it so offhandedly, I almost didn't hear. But I heard.

"Just about," Ed said. It was five-forty.

"The Compazine first, right?" she said.

I nodded. She turned toward her night table and picked up a bottle of tablets. "It's right here," she said. Of course it was. Along with the other things she would need—a small bottle of club soda and a glass. She had set the table, as always, in advance.

I watched her hands opening the bottle of Compazine. "One, right?"

I nodded again. She swallowed it expertly, back of the tongue, without water. She lay back on the pillow and closed her eyes. I had two simultaneous thoughts: It's started, and It's not too late to stop. It's only Compazine. She doesn't have to go on. She can stop.

She is up now, shuffling slowly toward the linen closet. Ed gets up to help her, but she shakes her head. "Sit," she says. Her cotton flannel nightgown—a pretty new one, white with small flowers—reaches to her ankles. Her feet are bare—her pale, chunky, baby feet, noiseless as they move across the carpet. She holds the wall as she goes and we watch her as if we are in a theater, part of a darkened audience focused on the single performer onstage. Finally, she reaches her destination, pulls open the closet door, and reaches inside. Now she turns and begins the walk back, the bottle of pills in her right hand. She holds the bottle up, as if it's a small torch lighting her way.

She sits on the side of her bed and places the bottle down on the night table next to the soda and the glass. "I forgot a bottle opener."

"I'll get it," says my husband, halfway there when she stops him.

"Sit down, Ed, please," she says in her teacher's voice. "I don't want you to touch anything." I open my mouth. And close it, pressing my lips together. She is up again, moving now toward the kitchen. She reappears, holding a bottle opener. When she reaches the bed, she sits down and places the opener on the table with the rest of the equipment.

"Is it time?"

"Not quite, Ida," my husband says almost inaudibly. This is going to happen. This is really going to happen.

My mother props up the pillows, then eases herself under the covers, smoothing down her nightgown as she lies back. She looks dreamily out the window and sighs. "I would have liked to die with my hair."

I sit on the edge of the bed and take her hand and kiss the back of it, not trusting myself to speak.

"Is it time now?" she asks. (Mommy, are we almost there?) Five-fifty-eight. The answer to her question is in my brain and my brain has instructed my vocal cords to deliver the answer, but my vocal cords are not delivering. My mother looks at me, senses the difficulty, bends forward to look at the clock, and answers the question herself. "Yes," she says, as if the end of the evening has come and the party is over, "it's time."

She sits up and takes the bottle of Nembutal in her hand. She opens the bottle and carefully taps its contents onto an indented place on the blanket. She puts the bottle down. The windows are tightly shut and, except for the small flapping sound of the digital clock passing from one minute to the next, the room is silent. She turns back toward the table and grasps the bottle of soda water in her left hand and the opener in her right. She tries to open the bottle and fails.

Ed gets to his feet and reaches toward her. "Please let me help you, Ida," he says in an unsteady voice.

She shakes her head. "I don't want you to touch anything. I can do it." And after another try, she does. The water fizzes as she pours it into the glass. She leans over in the direction of her knees and looks down at the small pile of shiny capsules lying like candies on the yellow blanket. She picks up two or three of them in her fingers, places them on her tongue, lifts the glassful of soda water and, with a short swig, swallows them, then three more. Then three more. Soon she falls into a rhythm—pick them up, toss them on the tongue, lift the glass, swallow; pick them up, toss them on the tongue . . .

"You're doing it, Mother," I whisper. "You're doing it. You're doing great." I am on my feet now. My hands are crossed and flattened on my chest as if to keep my heart from bursting through my chest wall. The play on stage has turned into a sports event. My mother is performing the decathlon.

I want to jump out of my stone encasement and cheer. I want to wave a flag, blow a horn, scream, weep, cry, shout. Hooray for you, Mother! You're doing it, Mother! You're doing it just right! You're—

She has stopped. The dent in the blanket where the

capsules once were is empty. There are no more capsules. Half to herself, she says, "Now the Dalmane."

There are only five of these and she downs them in two swallows. Someone in my head screams. Ed, I know, is behind me. I know if I reach my arm straight back I will touch his arm, but my arm doesn't move because my body, like my vocal cords, seems bolted in place. My mother straightens the bedcovers and smooths her pillow and lies back, all in slow motion. The room has darkened, except for the pool of light from the bedside lamp, which shines on her as if she were an oil painting. We enter the light, my husband and I, and we take our places on either side of her as if in a ceremony. We each take one of her hands and for a moment we are all perfectly, harmoniously still. Then my mother begins to speak in a way that sounds like a chant:

"I want you to know that I am a happy woman. I made a man happy for forty years, and I gave birth to the most wonderful child, and late in life I had another child whom I love as if I had given birth to him too. No one has been more blessed than I. I've had a wonderful life. I've had everything that is important to me. I have given love and I have received it. No one is more grateful than—"

She stops suddenly and opens her eyes. "I'm not sleepy."

It's as if someone has switched off the music and flipped on the lights. "You will be, Mother," I hear myself say, as my spine straightens and my blood turns to ice. "It doesn't work right away. Just close your eyes and relax. We're here. Everything's going to be all right. You did it. You did it just right. Close your eyes. Relax. Don't worry. We're here. We love you . . ."

Please let it work. Please. Please.

"You'll soon be asleep," whispers Ed. "You'll sleep peacefully."

"Oh yes, I'm starting to feel it now. Oh, good. Remember, I am the most happy woman. And this is my wish. I want you to remember ..."

"I love you, Mother!" I call to her, "I love you," and when she does not answer, I lower my face into the soft flesh of her neck. Now the cement that has been holding me together begins to crack. I stumble backwards, collapse into a chair and with both hands clamped over my mouth, I sob. I sob heavily, but not for long. Because when I look up and see how still she is, I know that she has found the door she was looking for and that it has closed, gently, behind her.

ABOUT THE AUTHOR

BETTY ROLLIN, journalist, TV newswoman and best-selling author, is a correspondent for NBC News and has worked for ABC News as a contributing correspondent for "Nightline." A former editor and writer at *Vogue* and *Look*, she has written numerous articles for national publications including *The New York Times*. The acclaimed author of two autobiographical books, *First, You Cry* and *Am I Getting Paid for This?*, she lives with her husband, a mathematician, in Manhattan.